PELICAN BOOKS

A537

THE ECONOMIC HISTORY OF WORLD POPULATION

CARLO M. CIPOLLA

CARLO M. CIPOLLA

THE ECONOMIC HISTORY OF
WORLD POPULATION

PENGUIN BOOKS

Penguin Books Ltd, Harmondsworth, Middlesex
U.S.A.: Penguin Books Inc., 3300 Clipper Mill Road, Baltimore 11, Md
AUSTRALIA: Penguin Books Pty Ltd, 762 Whitehorse Road,
Mitcham, Victoria

—

First published 1962

—

Copyright © Carlo M. Cipolla, 1962

—

Made and printed in Great Britain
by Hazell Watson & Viney Ltd
Aylesbury and Slough
Set in Linotype Times Roman

Manlio, dilectissimo fratri,
probo viro necnon
medico praeclaro,
in omni parte humanitatis
versato

D.D.D.

Contents

List of Text Figures

List of Tables

LIST OF TABLES

Preface

FAST and cheap transportation has been one of the main products of the Industrial Revolution. Distances have been shortened at an astonishing pace. Day by day the world seems smaller and smaller and societies that for millennia practically ignored each other are suddenly put in contact – or in conflict. In our dealings, in politics as in economics, in health organization as in military strategy, a new point of view is forced upon us. Somewhere in the past people had to move from an urban or regional point of view to a national one. Today we have to adjust ourselves and our way of thinking to a *global* point of view. As Bertrand Russell recently wrote, 'The world has become one not only for the astronomer but for the ordinary citizen.'

This book attempts to describe from a global point of view the development of mankind in its material endeavour: its growth in numbers and levels of living. From the same global point of view, I have tried to touch upon some of the alarming problems that mankind is facing today: the population explosion, the growing need for energy resources, the diffusion of technical knowledge, and the role of education in an industrial society.

Writing this book has been a most ambitious task; but I could count on the help of learned friends and colleagues whom I exploited with indecent pertinacity. Among the more illustrious victims I must remember Miss Phyllis Deane, Gregory Grossman, Alexander Gershenkron, Harvey Leibenstein, Martin Hofbaum, and Henry Rosovsky. Adam Pepelasis and George Richardson read the manuscript in its entirety and gave me all kinds of valuable criticisms and

PREFACE

suggestions. My friends John Gawthrey and John Scott, and my students Victoria Chick, Elizabeth Conner, Walter Abbott, Harold Jackson, and Hans Palmer helped me with linguistic problems. My secretary Franca Zennaro is unduly convinced that the age of slavery is not yet over. To all of them I want to express my gratitude while reassuring them with the statement that no one of them is to be held responsible for any of the views expressed in this book.

CARLO M. CIPOLLA

Berkeley Calif.
October 1960

Acknowledgements

I AM indebted to many publishers and authors for permission to quote passages and reprint figures. In particular I have to acknowledge my grateful indebtedness to the following:

Abelard-Schuman Ltd of London for permission to quote a passage from *Man the Maker* by R. J. Forbes (London–New York, 1958); the Cambridge University Press for permission to quote a passage from *The Neolithic Cultures of the British Isles* by S. Piggott (Cambridge, 1954); Doubleday & Co. of New York for granting me permission to quote a passage from *Back of History* by W. Howells (New York, 1954); Harper & Brothers of New York for permission to quote a passage from the *Adventures with the Missing Link* by R. A. Dart (New York, 1959); George G. Harrap & Co. of London and the Indiana University Press for granting me permission to reproduce figure 16 and figure 75 from *Power and Production* (*Energy for Man* in the American edition) by H. Thirring; Professor Dudley Kirk for permission to reproduce figure 46 from his book *Europe's Population in the Interwar Years* (New York, 1946); the *Saturday Review* for permission to quote from 'Education: The Long View' by A. J. Toynbee, which appeared in the issue of 19 November 1960; the Viking Press of New York for permission to quote a passage from *The Challenge of Man's Future* by H. Brown (New York, 1954).

CHAPTER 1

The Two Revolutions

THERE are nine major planets in the solar system. One of them is the earth. It is one of the nearest to the sun: one of the smallest, judging by its diameter: and one of those with the highest density, if not the one with the highest density of all.

The earth is covered with a thin film of matter called life. 'The film is exceedingly thin, so thin that its weight can scarcely be more than one-billionth [1000 millionth] that of the planet which supports it.... [It is] so insignificant in size that it would be detectable only with the greatest difficulty by beings on other planets, and would certainly be unnoticeable to observers elsewhere in our galaxy.... It is insubstantial, flaccid, and sensitive in the extreme so that a slight cosmic ripple would quickly bring destruction. Yet, in an ever-changing way, the envelope of living things has continued to exist for the greatest part of the earth's history.'[1]

'Man' is part of this thin, living envelope: but he represents a very late appearance. Vermes were already on the earth almost 450 million years ago, jawless fishes 400 million years, scorpions 350 million years, bony fishes 300 million years, amphibia 270 million years, reptilia 250 million years, winged insects 225 million years, grasshoppers 215 million years, birds 140 million years, marsupials 80 million years.[2] Man appeared in his present form possibly

1. Brown, 1954, p. 3. (See Bibliography for details of books mentioned in footnotes.)
2. Zeuner, 1958, p. 365.

17

less than half a million years ago. He appeared when many other species had already died out and when all the species that exist today had already been on the earth for a long, long time.

THE AGRICULTURAL REVOLUTION

For thousands and thousands of years, man lived as a predatory animal. Hunting, fishing, gathering wild fruits, and killing and eating other men remained for a very long time the only ways by which man could secure for himself the necessary means of subsistence. As a most ancient Sumerian text forcibly evoked, 'when the human species appeared, it did not know bread nor cloth. Man walked on hands and feet. He ate grass with the mouth as animals do, and he drank the water of the stream.'[1] In the course of time, particular skills and techniques were invented and developed, the cutting of stones, the making of special weapons, the building of transport devices, but everything remained in the general framework of a predatory economy. New skills and innovations merely helped to increase man's efficiency in hunting, fishing, and killing. 'Man lived as a really primitive hunter and gatherer of wild fruits and vegetables for all but one per cent of his known existence.'[2]

It was only very recently – somewhere, somehow – that the first great economic revolution came: the discovery of agriculture and the domestication of animals.

Excavations at Jericho, in the Dead Sea Valley of Palestine, have laid bare the remains of an ancient farming village. Radioactive carbon dates the village at around 7000 B.C.[3] The same excavations also brought to light materials

1. Quoted by Pirenne, 1950, Vol. 1, p. 4.
2. Howells, 1959, p. 143.
3. Zeuner, 1956, pp. 195–7; Kenyon, 1959, p. 7.

definitely belonging to a Mesolithic structure, i.e. preceding agriculture. The Mesolithic materials pre-date the Neolithic ones by about 800 years. The evidence would therefore indicate that 'the development from the Palestinian Mesolithic to a fully Neolithic type settlement took place at Jericho in a period covering approximately the eighth millennium B.C.'[1]

Excavations in the inward slopes of the Zagros mountain crescent in Kurdistan have provided evidence of two village farm communities at Jarmo in Iraq and at Tepe Sarab in Iran. These villages 'were apparently inhabited between 7000 and 6500 B.C.'[2] The people of the Jarmo area domesticated animals[3] and grew barley and two different kinds of wheat.[4] Other excavations at Karim Shahir and at M'lcefat seem to indicate that incipient agriculture was possibly practised in these places even earlier than at Jarmo.[5]

In Northern Iran, near the shore of the Caspian Sea, evidence of incipient agriculture was discovered by an expedition digging a site called Belt Cave. The people who lived in the cave around 6600 B.C. were still hunters. But at a date around 5800 B.C. people lived in the cave who domesticated goats and sheep. By 5300 B.C. the cave was certainly inhabited by people who had begun to make pottery and to reap grain as well as to keep pigs and, a little later, cows.[6]

1. Kenyon, 1959, p. 9. See also Kenyon, 1957, pp. 82–4, and Gordon Childe, 1958, pp. 35–6.

2. Braidwood, 1960, p. 136. In his previous work (1957) Professor Braidwood seemed to favour a somewhat later date for the appearance of agriculture in the Near East.

3. Certainly the goat. Possibly also horses, dogs, and cattle.

4. Braidwood, 1957, pp. 128–30.

5. ibid, pp. 112–27.

6. Coon, 1957, Chapter 4; 1958, p. 143.

All the available evidence seems therefore to indicate that the Agricultural Revolution occurred in the Near East sometime around the eighth millennium B.C.

On the American continent, recent archaeological ex-

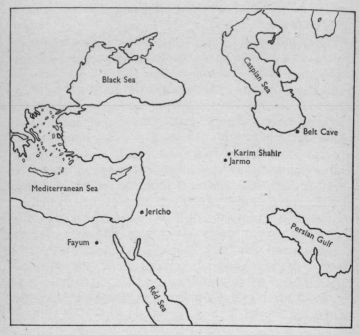

Fig. 1. The sites of incipient agriculture in the Near East

cavations in the Chicama and Viru Valleys of northern Peru have brought to light the remains of ancient farming communities belonging to a pre-ceramic culture that apparently did not know maize. On the basis of these discoveries Bird believes that agriculture in that area appeared around 2200

B.C.[1] Kroeber considers this estimate 'reasonable', but with the understanding that it can 'turn out to be half again too long or too short'.[2] Further north, in the Bat Cave in New Mexico, primitive cobs of domesticated maize have been dated by radiocarbon as *c.* 3650 B.C. Other cobs of cultivated primitive maize have been found in La Perra Cave in Mexico. Radiocarbon determinations of associated vegetal remains suggest a date, *c.* 2500 B.C.[3]

What was the origin of these developments? Was American agriculture introduced by Neolithic immigrants? Or was it the product of indigenous independent discovery? If the latter is the case, we are left with two independent nuclear areas of the Agricultural Revolution – the Near East and the American continent.

What, then, about the Far East? There is no doubt that the Neolithic Revolution spread eastward from the Near East. Before 3300 B.C. it had reached Beluchistan.[4] Did it stop at the Indus drainage area in India? Or did it extend its influence throughout Central Asia? In China and South-East Asia the Neolithic Revolution occurred after 5000 B.C.[5] Was it brought there by Neolithic immigrants from the West? Or was there an independent discovery of plant and animal domestication somewhere in the monsoon lands around the Gulf of Bengal or the South Chinese Sea? Should we admit a third independent nuclear area of the Revolution in South-East Asia?[6]

1. Bird, 1948, p. 28. See also Alden Mason, 1957, pp. 31–4.
2. Kroeber, 1948, p. 119.   3. Mangelsdorf, 1954, pp. 409 10.
4. Fairservis, 1956, p. 356.
5. Bishop, 1933, pp. 389–404; Fairservis, 1959, p. 139.
6. C. O. Sauer, 1952, maintains that South-East Asia was the most ancient cradle of the Neolithic Revolution and that all other developments were just a diffusional phenomenon. This thesis has been accepted by a few authors, but it is based on pure speculation and

We cannot answer these questions. Our ignorance is still too great. The first great step towards civilization remains a fascinating mystery in the story of man.

Nevertheless it is certain that some human groups in the Near East – around 7000 B.C. and possibly before – practised some agriculture and domesticated animals. It may be that these skills were known to other human groups in some other area of the world, but undoubtedly the greatest part of the human race was still living by hunting, fishing, and gathering. Henceforth, we witness the diffusion of the great Revolution. Careful and patient archaeological excavations allow us to follow pretty closely its advance from the Near East into Africa and Europe.

In the Nile Valley, excavations along the shore of Lake Fayum show remains of grain bins or silos dating from *c.* 4500 B.C. Creeping south along the Nile, the Revolution reached the Sudan possibly around 3500 B.C. and Kenya (Hyrax Hill) about 3000 B.C. This southward movement was slowed down if not altogether stopped by the great swamps behind the headwaters of the Nile.[1]

At the same time the Revolution spread into Europe. The Danube and the Mediterranean were the roads along which the new way of living invaded the West (Fig. 2). Between 4500 and 2000 B.C. an agricultural economy developed in

up to the present moment there is no archaeological evidence that substantiates it. P. G. Mangelsdorf reviewing Sauer's book in *American Antiquity*, 19 (1953), pp. 87–9, could justifiably complain that 'if one sought, as an exercise in imagination, to design a completely untestable theory of agricultural origins and dispersal, it would be difficult to improve upon it.' The very fact is that, as R. J. Braidwood and C. A. Reed (1957, p. 21) recently repeated, 'from Southern and South-Eastern Asia there is practically nothing archaeologically available at all.'

1. Braidwood, 1957, p. 135; Cole, 1954, pp. 216–17.

the lands now known as the Balkans, Switzerland, Germany, Denmark, Southern Sweden, Italy, France, and Spain. Later, it invaded the British Isles and Scandinavian areas. By 1500 B.C. the last European stronghold of the pure hunting

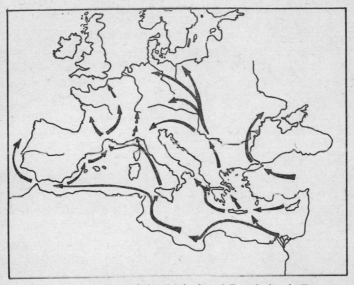

Fig. 2. The diffusion of the Agricultural Revolution in Europe
(based on Varagnac, 1959, p. 374)

economy was the zone of tundra and coniferous forest extending from the Norwegian coasts right across Northern Eurasia.[1]

In time the Agricultural Revolution spread all over the world. The hunters became 'marginal' in all senses of the

1. In general see Gordon Childe, 1958, especially Chapters 2 and 3; Piggott, 1954; Iversen, 1941; Nougier, 1950; Bailloud, 1955; Zeuner, 1958, pp. 72–109, and the important Scandinavian bibliography quoted and summarized in Zeuner's work.

word. 'Some were marginal in being remote and isolated literally at the world's ends: the Bushmen of South Africa, the natives of Australia, of the Andaman Islands in the Bay of Bengal and of the Tierra del Fuego at the bottom of South America. Most have been marginal in their resources and territory and have survived to this day because what they had no one else wanted, such as the last Bushman stronghold in the Kalahari Desert or the barren ground and arctic parts of Siberia and America.' [1]

By A.D. 1780 the hunting stage had already long since been abandoned by nearly all mankind. And the 'farmers' were definitely irrupting into the few strongholds of the last paleolithic and mesolithic hunters.

THE INDUSTRIAL REVOLUTION

Then, late in the eighteenth century, the second Revolution was born: the Industrial Revolution. England was its cradle. Its diffusion was rapid. By 1850 it had largely penetrated into France and Belgium. By 1900 it had reached Germany, Sweden, the United States, Northern Italy, Russia, and Japan. Now, it is spreading into India, China, South America, and Africa (Fig. 3).

Wherever the Industrial Revolution penetrated, it brought into the entire structure of the society a general aggregate of changes that made industry, instead of agriculture, the predominant productive sector of the society. The advance of the farmers was halted and indeed transformed into a rapid retreat. The proportion of the world's active population engaged in agriculture was most probably above 80 per cent in 1750. It was around 60 per cent in

1. Howells, 1954, p. 120.

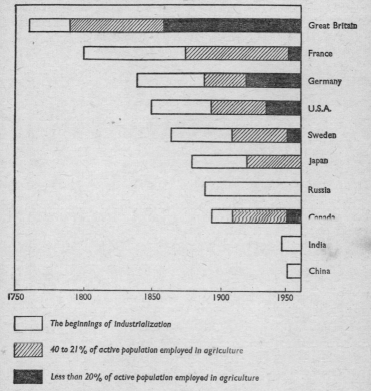

Fig. 3. The diffusion of the Industrial Revolution

1950 (see Tables 1 and 2). And it continues to fall at an extraordinary pace (see Fig. 3).[1] The day may not be too distant when the proportion of farmers in the world will be no larger than the proportion of hunters in the late eighteenth century.

1. For the demographic aspects of the phenomenon see Davis, 1951, pp. 8–19.

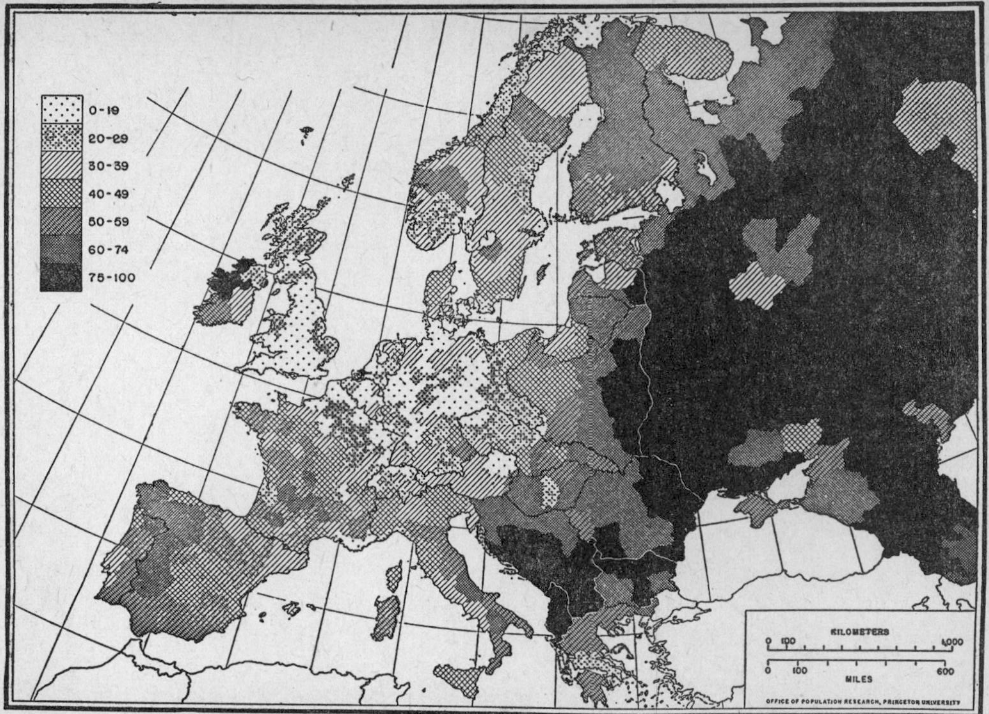
0-19
20-29
30-39
40-49
50-59
60-74
75-100
KILOMETERS
0 100 1,000
0 100 600
MILES
OFFICE OF POPULATION RESEARCH, PRINCETON UNIVERSITY

Fig. 4. Per cent of population dependent on agriculture in Europe, by minor divisions, about 1930 (from Kirk, 1945)

Though industry now tends to predominate, we cannot say that the world tends to be populated by industrial workers. Most of the active members of an agricultural society are engaged in agricultural pursuits. In an industrial society a much smaller proportion, 30 to 50 per cent, is actually employed in 'industry'. Instead, a good deal of the rest are employed in a varied set of activities like government, banking, insurance, the liberal professions, and all sorts of service-producing business that economists and

TABLE 1. *Percentage of active population employed in agriculture in selected countries, 1850, 1900, and 1950*

	About 1850	About 1900	About 1950
AFRICA			
Egypt		70	65
French Morocco			67
South Africa		60	49
AMERICA			
Argentina			25
Brazil			61
Canada		42	20
Mexico		70	61
U.S.A.	65	38	13
ASIA			
China			70
Japan		70	49
India			74
Malaya			52
Pakistan			80
Thailand			86
EUROPE			
Austria			33
Belgium		20	12
Czechoslovakia			38
Denmark		38	22
France	55	43	30
Germany		35	24
Great Britain	22	9	5

TABLE 1 (*continued*). *Percentage of active population employed in agriculture in selected countries, 1850, 1900, and 1950*

EUROPE	About 1850	About 1900	About 1950
Greece			54
Ireland		45	40
Italy		60	42
Low Countries		30	20
Norway		41	21
Poland		77	53
Portugal			47
Spain			50
Sweden		40	21
Switzerland		30	16
Turkey			86
Yugoslavia			70
OCEANIA			
Australia		25	22
New Zealand		30	18
U.S.S.R.	85	80	45

statisticians, for want of a better term, call the 'tertiary sector'.[1] Further development of 'automation' will probably further reduce the proportion of the active population actually engaged in 'industry'. From a purely occupational point of view, it will be probably true to say that *'rien ne sera moins industriel que la civilisation née de la Revolution Industrielle'*.[2]

WHAT SORT OF REVOLUTION?

Historians have too often overemphasized the changes that constantly occur in history by labelling them 'Revolutions'. They detected an 'Urban Revolution' in early historic times, a 'Commercial Revolution' in eleventh-century Europe, a

1. On the concept of 'tertiary sector' see Clark, 1957; Bauer and Yamey, 1951, pp. 741–55; Minkes, 1955, pp. 366–73.
2. Fourastié, 1949, p. 74.

'sort of Industrial Revolution' in eleventh-century Holland, and an 'Industrial Revolution' in thirteenth-century England. But from our point of view, at least, all these 'Revolutions' were scarcely revolutionary. They brought some changes, but they did not alter the fundamental economic character of the societies involved. When the first 'towns' appeared, the societies experiencing the new phenomenon continued to be fundamentally agricultural and the 'towns' were mere organs of a more complex agricultural world – often nothing more than collecting centres of agricultural rents. As Professor Frankfort has pointed out 'the great divergence between city and countryside, between rural and urban life is, in the form in which we are familiar with it, a product of the industrial revolution'.[1] Similarly, the enthusiasm and skill displayed by medievalists in describing merchants, bankers, textile manufacturers, and town-life mostly had the effect of concealing from the average cultivated person – and often from the medievalists themselves – that even the most highly developed European societies of the Middle Ages remained fundamentally agrarian. The fraction of the active population and resources engaged in trade and manufacture was small, most of the trade itself was connected with agricultural products, the famous merchants and bankers were generally part-time landlords (as most of the artisans and sailors were part-time peasants) and finally – as we shall see later by far the greatest part of the energy used was actually derived from agriculture.

The Agricultural Revolution of the eighth millennium B.C. and the Industrial Revolution of the eighteenth century A.D., on the other hand, created deep breaches in the continuity of the historical process. With each one of these two Revolutions, a 'new story' begins: a new story dramatically

1. Frankfort, 1951, p. 57.

and completely alien to the previous one. Continuity is broken between the cave-man and the builders of the pyramids, just as all continuity is broken between the ancient ploughman and the modern operator of a power station.

In this context the term 'Revolution' is certainly not in-

TABLE 2. *Percentage of active population employed in agriculture by continents, 1950*

	Total population (millions)	Active population (millions)	Active population employed in agriculture (percentage)
AFRICA			
North Africa	65	24	73
Tropical and South Africa	132	65	76
Total	197	89	75
AMERICA			
North America	166	66	13
Middle America	51	18	62
South America	110	41	55
Total	327	125	34
ASIA			
South West	41	13	70
South Central	460	173	74
South East	170	65	78
East	698	277	71
Total	1369	528	73
EUROPE			
North and West	198	90	20
Central	88	42	47
Southern	128	58	58
Total	414	190	38
OCEANIA	13	5	17
U.S.S.R.	195	88	45
WORLD	2515	1025	59

Source: I.L.O., 1956, p. 557.

tended to mean that the changes involved represented sudden accidents unrelated to previous situations and evolutions. It is all too clear today that the Industrial Revolution was the product of cultural, social, and economic changes that had occurred in the British Isles between 1550 and 1780.[1] And though we know almost nothing about the origin of the Agricultural Revolution, we are convinced that the way was paved by changes in 'the level of culture' as well as in the 'natural condition of the environment'.[2] Each 'Revolution' had its roots in the past. But each 'Revolution' created a deep break with the very same past. The first 'Revolution' transformed hunters and food-gatherers into farmers and shepherds. The second one transformed farmers and shepherds into operators of 'mechanical slaves' fed with inanimate energy.

1. Among many others see Nef, 1954.
2. Braidwood, 1957, p. 100, and 1960, p. 134.

CHAPTER 2

The Sources of Energy

MAN has 'needs'. He has basic physiological needs, like food and drink. He has other elementary needs, like clothing and heating. Finally he has, as it were, 'high standard' needs, like reading, listening to music, travelling, amusing himself. Human needs have no upper limit, but they have a lower limit: the minimum food necessary to maintain life.

The nature, magnitude, and form of human needs vary with cultural and geophysical environments, with class, with age, body size, sex, type, and degree of activity. The range of differentiation is indeed wide for the less elementary needs. But even for the very elementary ones there are noticeable differences. Of two populations with the same age structure and average body size, one living at a mean annual temperature of 25° C. will need about seven per cent fewer calories than an equivalent population living at a mean temperature of 10° C. The influence of body size is such that, other things being equal, a population in which the average male adult weighs 65 kilograms will need about fifteen per cent more calories than a population in which the average man weighs only 50 kilograms. At the same body weight, adult females require about twenty per cent fewer calories than adult males of the same age. It is also estimated that among adults of the same size, the caloric need declines at the rate of about five per cent for each decade after the age of thirty.[1]

Man satisfies his various needs in vastly different ways, using an extremely varied 'basket' of commodities and ser-

1. Keys, 1958, pp. 28–9.

vices – bread, meat, wine, milk, cotton, wool, fuel, paper, steel, electricity, gas, and so on. One way of keeping an account in real terms of such an extraordinarily heterogeneous 'basket' is to refer to the energy value of each item. The unit of account generally used is the 'calorie'. A 'calorie' represents the equivalent of the amount of heat required to raise the temperature of one kilogram of water by one degree centigrade. For conversion into electricity equivalents, the conventional ratio of approximately 860 calories to one kilowatt hour is generally adopted.

Despite its apparent simplicity, this system of account is somewhat problematical. It contains all sorts of obstacles and traps and can be dealt with only by allowing a considerable margin of approximation. One of the main sets of difficulties is afforded by the conversion of equivalents. As will be readily appreciated, their assessment involves arbitrary calculations in the attempt to express one form of energy in terms of another, to evaluate average efficiencies and load factors of major applications, and to rate the horsepower of machines in service.

Man needs energy. But man himself produces energy. The chemical energy with which man is fuelled is partly transformed by him into mechanical energy in the form of muscular work. Actually, most of his energy intake is lost in the form of heat, part is used in chemical processes, and part (about 10 per cent) leaves the body as waste product. Only a minor portion finally appears as nervous and mechanical activity. We cannot measure the energy value of the nervous activity,[1] but we can evaluate approximately

1. But we can evaluate its 'cost', i.e. the energy input it requires. In fact it is commonly estimated that mental work requires an approximate specific energy expenditure of seven to eight calories per hour.

the energy value of the mechanical activity. It has been calculated that the average efficiency of the human body as a machine varies from 10 to 25 per cent depending on the type of work, the speed with which it is done, and the skill and training of the individual doing it. Mechanical efficiency of muscular work can be markedly affected by training. Improvements as great as 37 per cent are quoted in the scientific literature. But it is generally admitted that for sustained work the maximum of human efficiency to be expected is about 18 per cent of the energy input.[1]

Man can use his energy output to master and utilize other forms of energy. The more successfully he does so, the more he acquires control over his environment and achieves goals other than those strictly related to animal existence.[2]

THE CONVERSION OF ENERGY

Energy is available to man when he comes to know about its sources and is capable of mastering them in an economical way. Here, one of the main problems is how to transform energy into particular forms at a particular time and place and at convenient cost.

To solve this problem man must make use of various types of converters. A steam engine, for instance, is a converter. It transforms heat energy into mechanical energy when and where desired. It must be remembered that every transformation of energy involves consumption and losses. The output of useful energy (that is to say, into the final form required) obtained by transformation is always less than the energy input. The technical efficiency of a converter is

1. Amar, 1920, pp. 186–98; Pyke, 1950, p. 27.
2. For a broad approach to the subject see Ostwald, 1909; Zimmermann, 1951, Chapter 5; Cottrell, 1955.

determined by the arithmetical ratio between useful output and total input. Very often, various successive transformations are necessary to be able to obtain energy in the form and at the moment that it is required. This, naturally, involves successive losses which are determined by the rate of the technical efficiency of the various converters successively used.[1] For example, if 100 tons of coal are used to produce first steam and then electricity, the quantity of electricity produced can be divided by the quantity of energy equivalent to the coal employed and thus obtain, let us say, a rate of efficiency of 23 per cent. But to extract, work, carry, and use the hundred tons of coal energy, ten tons of coal, let us say, must be employed. Furthermore, the carrying of the electricity to the final converter involves losses, let us say 15 per cent. Finally, the transformation of the electricity into mechanical energy by the final converter causes further losses, let us say 10 per cent. The rate of technical efficiency of the whole system of these converters employed will be $\frac{100}{110} \times 0.23 \times 0.85 \times 0.90 = 16\%$.

The economic efficiency of a converter is measured by the cost per unit of useful energy that the converter produces in comparison with the cost per unit of useful energy produced by alternative converters. The cost of useful energy produced by a converter is determined by a complex of variables such as the technical efficiency of the converter, its cost of production, its durability and obsolescence, the cost of operating it, and the prevailing price of the source of energy it uses.

From our point of view, plants and edible animals also have to be considered as converters. Plants, through the pro-

1. C.E.C.A., 1957, pp. 14–15.

cess of photosynthesis, transform solar light, water, carbon dioxide, and minerals into organic materials containing in various proportions the three main components of human food, i.e. carbohydrates, proteins, and fats. In short, plants are essentially converters that transform sunlight into a form of chemical energy.

Edible animals are converters in so far as they transform one form of chemical energy into another that man finds more suitable or valuable. In fact, edible animals can assimilate plants or parts of plants that man cannot himself digest, and transform them into animal proteins and fats that he can assimilate. Furthermore, since animal proteins are of greater nutritive value than carbohydrates, man occasionally finds it convenient to use animals as converters even when he feeds them with plants that he could use directly.

From a purely technical point of view, animals and most plants are not very efficient converters.[1] As with man, most of the energy-input is actually used up by them in the process of staying alive. With animals, the loss is higher because of a cumulative process. By eating plants man gets only a fraction of their original energy input; by eating animals he gets only a fraction of the energy contained in the plants the animals had eaten, i.e. a fraction of a fraction of the energy input of the plants. The combined plant–animal converter, from the point of view of the quantity of energy produced, is less efficient because of a double loss. It has been calculated that, compared to corn production, beef production has only about ten per cent efficiency in land utilization for calories of energy. In other words, to

1. See the interesting 'Revenue and expenditure account for a leaf', calculated by Brown and Escombe, 'which shows so clearly the relative inefficiency of green plants'. Alsberg, 1948, pp. 130–32.

produce a given number of calories, beef needs ten times as much land as does corn. This is actually the fundamental reason why poor societies rely more on vegetable carbohydrates than on animal proteins. As to draught animals, it has been calculated that the mechanical energy they supply is only within the range of three to five per cent of the energy of the green fodder used to feed the animals.[1]

When *homo sapiens* appeared on the earth, he found plant and animal converters already in existence. For thousands and thousands of years – in fact for the greater part of his history – *homo sapiens* remained incapable of doing anything better than dashing all over the place trying to capture or to collect any edible plant or animal in sight. His knowledge was basically limited to what was edible and what was not.

Such a state of affairs cannot have been very comfortable. Man spent all his time and energy in the search for food, relying mainly on good luck and his ability to kill wild animals or other men. Starvation was a constant threat, forcing people to infanticide and cannibalism. Furthermore, since man had not yet learned to domesticate animals[2] and knew no other source of energy, his muscles were the only mechanical power he could command.

In a number of myths, animals are credited with having possessed fire before man. Fantastic as they seem, these myths probably contain a grain of truth. Modern archaeologists do not exclude the possibility that the sub-human Australopithecus mastered fire, though the matter is still open to discussion. Undoubted evidence of the use of fire comes from the cave of Choukoutien (China), where fossil

1. Baum, 1955, pp. 289–91.
2. With the exception of the dog, which was domesticated in Paleolithic times.

remains of a group of Sinanthropi have been found. This would prove that fire was mastered in Asia at some time between 450,000 and 350,000 B.C. In Europe the technique probably arrived later. The first sure indications came from English and Spanish archaeological sites dated around 250,000–200,000 B.C.[1]

Though fire was discovered very early, not all Paleolithic human groups came to know or take advantage of it. Some hunters used fire and some did not. It is also established that those who made use of fire in the most distant past used it only for warmth or for protection from predatory animals. Cooking was a development of the late Pleistocene.[2]

Fire allowed man to convert inedible plants to his use, thereby increasing the energy at his disposal. Use of this energy for warmth also allowed him to adventure into hitherto inhospitable areas.

In time, *homo sapiens* made progress in another direction. As indicated in the previous chapter, man perfected his hunting and killing techniques and developed special skills in working stone and preparing primitive tools.[3] In all these discoveries, however, including the use of fire, man merely increased his efficiency in exploiting the two groups of biological converters, plants and animals. Fundamentally he remained a parasite, though an increasingy efficient one.[4]

1. Oakley, 1955, pp. 36–48; Oakley, 1956, pp. 102–7. On the Australopithecus in particular see also Dart, 1959, pp. 156–8.
2. Coon, 1958, pp. 60–63.
3. For a first approach to the subject see Boraz, 1959, pp. 36–52. For further reading see the bibliography of the latter, pp. 104–6.
4. How efficient the 'parasite' could be is indicated by the size of animal ossuaries left by Paleolithic hunters. More than ten thousand horse skeletons have been counted at Solutré (France), and nearly a thousand mammoth skeletons have been found at Predmost (Czechoslovakia).

Parasitism carried with it its own danger that plants or animals might be destroyed more quickly than they could replace themselves. This danger increased the more efficiently the 'economic activity' of Paleolithic man was carried on. To break this bottleneck man had to learn how to control and increase the supply of plants and animals or to discover new sources of energy. These two problems were to be solved by the Agricultural and the Industrial Revolutions respectively.

THE AGRICULTURAL REVOLUTION

Indeed, the Agricultural Revolution consisted in the very process whereby man came to control and increase the supply of disposable plants and animals.

As indicated in Chapter 1, we do not know why or how this Revolution came about. We know that it developed after the end of the last glaciation. It is highly probable that climatic changes played their part. It is also reasonable to suppose that the people who first started to domesticate plants and animals must have developed powers of observation and experimentation. In all likelihood some cultural developments preceded the Agricultural Revolution.

We are on firmer ground when we try to assess the main consequences of the Revolution. Developing control of the supply of the two groups of biological converters – plants and animals – meant first of all the possibility of a much larger and more dependable supply of food. Furthermore, the domestication of animals meant that man could put some of them to work, thereby creating a completely new supply of mechanical energy.

39

In this way, new opportunities were suddenly presented. The total amount of energy that the human species could dispose of – chemical energy from edible plants and animals, heat from plants, power from draught animals – increased in proportions inconceivable to the old Paleolithic societies. Populations expanded in size beyond any former 'ceiling'. Villages sprang up and community life emerged. Accumulation of a social surplus became possible. Certain groups and classes at least became free of the continuous search for food. Specialization became possible and also higher forms of activity and leisurely speculation. To use a term generally adopted by archaeologists and anthropologists, the stage of 'savagery' was over.[1]

The ten millennia or so that separate the beginning of the Agricultural Revolution from the beginning of the Industrial Revolution witnessed a great number of discoveries and innovations that increased man's control over energy sources.

There were endless improvements in agriculture. New kinds of plants were domesticated. Plants already domesticated were diffused and acclimatized to various climates and soils. And in this very process, all were improved.[2] A good example is offered by maize, which in six thousand years or less evolved from a small wild grass bearing tiny ears no larger than a modern strawberry into one of the world's most productive cereals.[3]

At the same time, special tools and techniques were invented. Sometime between 6000 and 3000 B.C. the plough

1. Among others see Gordon Childe, 1958, p. 34; Burkitt, 1956, p. 245.
2. For the period 1100 B.C. to A.D. 565 see the information collected by Heichelheim, 1956, pp. 318–58.
3. Mangelsdorf, 1954, p. 410.

and the hoe-stick were developed.[1] The prehistoric and ancient oriental plough-shares were made of wood and could not be worked in other than so-called 'light soils'. But soon the technique of working metals was discovered. By 3000 B.C. iron ores were occasionally smelted in Mesopotamia. Iron objects dated 3000 B.C. have been found in Sumerian Ur and in Middle Egypt. After 1400 B.C. iron was smelted and worked on a large scale. The adoption and the diffusion of the iron plough-shares and other new metallic agricultural tools, opened 'heavy soils' to cultivation. The Greek and Italian civilizations would not have been possible without these developments.

Discoveries and advances were also made in irrigation, artificial fertilization, and land rotation. Three-field crop rotation was probably already known in classical Greece as early as the fourth century B.C.[2] All these developments were refined through the centuries, in classical and medieval times, by different societies according to the particular needs and requirements of the various environments. It was a slow but irresistible accumulation of knowledge, enriched day by day by experience and practical observation and transmitted from generation to generation, from region to region.

On the other hand, parallel developments occurred in man's exploitation of the 'non-sapientes' living creatures. More animals were domesticated, improved by hybridization, and diffused over larger geographical areas. Furthermore, important progress was accomplished in putting to

1. On the history of the digging stick, the hoe, the plough, and various agricultural techniques see, among others, the very good pages of Forde, 1955, pp. 378–93 and 432–7.

2. Heichelheim, 1956, p. 326. On the discovery and the diffusion of the technique of working iron see also Forde, 1955, pp. 384–8.

use the mechanical energy of draught animals. The discovery of the wheel, the technique of harnessing, and the invention of the horse-shoe were events of paramount importance.

We do not know exactly when the wheel was discovered. But we do know that wheeled vehicles were used by the Sumerians around 3500 B.C. In the Indus Valley wheeled carts were known by 2500 B.C. and their use spread into Egypt towards the middle of the second millennium B.C.[1] But the forward steering was not discovered until the fourteenth century of our era.[2] And in any case carts could not be extensively used for transportation before a very good network of roads had appeared.

Very early, and certainly before 3000 B.C., man also learned how to harness horses and oxen to carts and ploughs. This was indeed a great step in making use of the mechanical energy of draught animals. Yet the technique of harnessing remained very crude and extremely inefficient throughout classical times. Horses and oxen were then harnessed by a yoke resting on the withers. A strap attached to the yoke above the withers passed around the animal's neck. When the horse leaned forward to pull, the strap cut into its wind-pipe, hampered its breathing, and reduced its power. Another way of harnessing oxen was by tying the yoke to the horns, but this technique was also rather inefficient, for it put the neck of the animal under a well-nigh intolerable strain.

The drawbacks were overcome with the development of a rigid collar resting on the shoulders of the animal. It seems that this harness was invented by the Chinese in the fourth century B.C., but it did not appear in Europe before the sixth

1. Woolley, 1929, pp. 39, 50; Gordon Childe, 1955, p. 101.
2. Gille, 1956, p. 79.

century A.D. Actually in Western Europe as late as the twelfth century A.D. it had not completely supplanted the old harness.[1]

Another important contribution was the discovery of the horse-shoe. Recent excavations in Austria seem to prove that the horse-shoe was invented by the Celtic inhabitants of the Alps about 400 B.C.,[2] but it became widely adopted in Western Europe only very much later. Without it a horse or ox working on hard and rocky ground wore out its feet rapidly, and a minor foot injury might permanently disable an otherwise useful and healthy animal. The introduction of iron shoes, attached by nails, made both horse and oxen much more efficient and durable.

Mention should also be made here of tools such as the lever, the hammer, the tongs, the saw, the potter's wheel, the loom, the various types of gears, etc. The discovery of such tools and their improvements remain unfortunately anonymous and belong to the most shadowy chapter of history. But they were of great importance in improving man's use of his own energy.

All that has been said illustrates the fundamental character of the developments that occurred in the period between the Agricultural and the Industrial Revolutions. Such developments were increasing the efficiency of the plant and animal converters, either by improving and adapting them to various environments or by finding more efficient ways of using them. Indeed it seems as if the human species spent

1. Lefebvre des Noèttes, 1931; Bloch, 1935, pp. 634–43; Haudri-court, 1936, pp. 515–22; White, 1940, pp. 141–59; Gille, 1956, p. 78. Burdford, 1960, pp. 1–18, maintains however that the old harness, although unsuited to the horse, was suited to the ox.
2. Heichelheim, 1956, p. 325.

centuries and millennia in improving the basic Neolithic discovery.

There were some exceptions to this general trend. The most important were the water-mill, the windmill, and the sailing boat.

The water-mill already existed by Augustus's time, and probably half a century earlier. But at least two centuries seem to have elapsed after its invention before it began to be generally adopted.[1] One possible reason for this failure is that classical society had abundance of alternative energy in the form of slave labour and animal power. Actually, it was only when slave labour grew scarce that the water-mill was adopted throughout Western Europe. Medieval and modern times witnessed its triumph.[2] In medieval Europe water-mills were no longer used only for grinding grain and pressing olives but were also applied to other productive activities such as cloth and paper making, and iron production.[3] The use of the water-mills in cloth production accounted for an extraordinary growth in textile manufacturing in thirteenth-century England.[4]

The windmill was known in the Near and Far East already in classical times. It became widely used in Europe only after the close of the twelfth century.[5]

Sailing boats appeared very early, and were soon adopted over much of the world. The first known indication of their existence is preserved in the British Museum. On a pre-dynastic vase of Amratian style from Middle Egypt we find depicted something that is undoubtedly a sailing boat. The date of the vase is probably about 3500 B.C. There is also

1. Moritz, 1958, pp. 134–9.
2. Bloch, 1935, pp. 538–63; Gille, 1956, pp. 67–9.
3. Gille, 1954, pp. 1–15.
4. Carus-Wilson, 1941, pp. 39–50.
5. Usher, 1959, pp. 172–3.

plenty of evidence to indicate that sailing boats were plying the Eastern Mediterranean by 3000 B.C.[1]

The discovery and diffusion of these three converters – the water-mill, the windmill, and the sailing boat – allowed man to harness the energy in water and wind. The boat especially proved capable of great contributions to economic growth. It was not as the result of pure accident that all the great civilizations of the past developed near navigable rivers or on the shores of small, internal, easily navigable seas.

Nevertheless, the importance of the three new converters must not be exaggerated. We have already noticed that until recently man failed to make extensive use of water-mills and windmills. Even when these two converters became more generally favoured, their technical characteristics severely restricted their adoption to certain geographical areas and to particular sectors of economic activity. The boat had a much wider range of possibilities. But until the late fifteenth century A.D., navigation, partly because of technical reasons and partly because of defensive needs, continued to rely heavily on manpower, while using the sail only as a complementary and secondary source of energy.[2]

One should probably note in passing that, since very ancient times, coal, asphalt, oil, and natural gas had occasionally been used as fuel for heating and lighting in specific areas. However, these were definitely isolated and exceptional cases and their relevance in the overall supply of energy remained quite negligible.

In conclusion, it is safe to say that until the Industrial

1. Barnett, 1958, pp. 220–30; Le Baron Bowen, 1960, pp. 117–31.
2. One may remember the Phoenician and Roman galleys, the Viking boat, the medieval Mediterranean galley, and the Polynesian sailing canoe.

Revolution man continued to rely mainly on plants and animals for energy – plants for food and fuel, and animals for food and mechanical energy. The use of other available sources – mainly wind and water power – remained definitely limited. There is no evidence that makes possible a precise quantitative assessment, but on the basis of general traits one may probably venture to say that eighty to eighty-five per cent of the total energy income at any time before the Industrial Revolution must have been derived from plants, animals, and men.

Obviously the exact proportion in which wind and water supplemented the other basic sources of energy varied from society to society and from time to time. The degree of efficiency with which all available sources were exploited also varied in the same way. Cultural patterns and institutions, levels of technology, conditions of war or peace, and geophysical environment were responsible for these differences. Whatever the reasons, the *per capita* availability of energy must have varied markedly from one agricultural society to another. One needs no particular arguments to be convinced that the average *per capita* consumption of energy in Western Europe must have been much higher during the thirteenth century than during the seventh or that the average Roman of the first century A.D. must have controlled much more energy (without taking slave labour into account) than any early Neolithic cultivator of Jarmo in the fifth millennium B.C.

Yet, the fact that the main sources of energy other than man's muscular work remained basically plants and animals must have set a limit to the possible expansion of the energy supply in any given agricultural society of the past. The limiting factor in this regard is ultimately the supply of land.

It is impossible – not to say irrelevant – to calculate what could have been the theoretical maximum *per capita* supply of energy in an agricultural society before the Industrial Revolution with an optimum state of technology, optimum distribution of income, optimum cultural and social environment, optimum supply of capital, and so forth. But a very rough estimate of the historical maximum is probably not impossible. In fact, if one considers contemporary agricultural societies – where, to some extent, the use of new sources of energy has been developed – one may venture to say that, apart from a few primitive tribes that carried to an incredible extent the practice of burning wood, most of the agricultural societies of the past must generally have had an overall *per capita* consumption of energy below 15,000 calories per day – possibly less than 10,000. And most of the actual consumption was put to food and warmth. The diffusion of slavery was just one of the consequences of this general scarcity of other forms of available energy.

THE INDUSTRIAL REVOLUTION

If the Agricultural Revolution is the process whereby man came to control and increase the supply of biological converters (plants and animals), the Industrial Revolution can be regarded as the process whereby the large scale exploitation of new sources of energy by means of inanimate converters was set on foot. Looking at things from this point of view, one easily understands the key role played by the so-called 'scientific revolution' of the sixteenth and seventeenth centuries in the shaping of the destiny of mankind.[1] It was, in fact, the 'scientific revolution' that gave to man

1. An excellent account of the scientific developments after 1500 is given by Hall, 1954.

the conceptual tools which enabled him to master new sources of energy. The conscious systematic investigation of phenomena revealed in man's environment had become a fundamental cultural trait of early modern Europe since the days of the Renaissance. In England these cultural developments happened to coincide with a shortage of a traditional form of energy (timber), the presence of large supplies of coal, and the existence of very active entrepreneurial groups created by a prolonged growth of commercial and maritime activities. It was – as W. S. Jevons once wrote – the 'union of certain happy mental qualities with material resources of an altogether peculiar character' that provided the explosive formula.

It all started with steam. 'Steam is an Englishman', as the old saying goes. In the second half of the eighteenth century, James Watt perfected previous discoveries and constructed a steam engine with technical and economic characteristics that led to its wide adoption. He began his experiments around 1765. Commercial use came after 1785 and to a greater extent after 1820. Steam engines were used in metallurgical and textile activities as well as in mining coal and in surface transportation. Actually more machine power made it possible to produce more coal and to transport it at an enormously accelerated rate. In its turn, more coal meant more machine power.

Coal became a strategic element in the emergence and diffusion of the industrial civilization. It meant a rapidly expanding supply of energy that could be used for heating and lighting and for power in sea and land transportation and in almost all the various forms of industry.

Around 1800 the world production of coal amounted to about fifteen million tons per annum. By 1860 it amounted to about 132 million tons per annum with an energy equivalent of about 1057 million megawatt-hours. By 1900, the production had increased to about 701 million tons with an energy equivalent of about 5606 million megawatt-hours. By 1950 the corresponding figures were 1454 million tons and 11,632 million megawatt-hours (Table 3).

A cumulative interaction was soon set in motion. The extraordinary growth in the supply of energy stimulated economic growth, which in turn stimulated education and scientific research leading to the discovery of new sources of energy.

In 1850 James Young, a Scottish chemist, established the basis for the making of petrol. About thirty-five years later, in Germany, Benz's and Daimler's motor-cars took successfully to the roads.

At the same time, Faraday's researches in electricity began to attract more and more attention. Progress in this field was rapid. By 1870 practical types of generators were already available producing either direct or alternating current. In those years Edison invented the incandescent lamp. 'At the Vienna Exhibition of 1883, practically all the electric appliances of modern life, such as electric hotplates, pans, cushions, and sheets were shown, but the great consumption of electricity was due to the evolution of the incandescent lamp. It stimulated the growth of network distribution and the production of huge quantities of electricity in power-plants, lowering the cost per kilowatt-hour until other electrical appliances became economical to use.'[1]

Under the impact of all these discoveries, the process quickened. The more energy produced, the more energy was sought. Man turned to the sun, the tides, earth-heat, tropical waters, and atmospheric electricity. Then, toward the middle of the twentieth century, he demonstrated that energy could

1. Forbes, 1958, p. 292.

TABLE 3. *World production of inanimate energy, 1860–1950*

Year	Coal	Lignite	Petrol-eum	Natural gasoline	Natural gas (milliard m³)	Water power (million megawatt -hours)	Total
	(million of tons)						
1860	132	6	—	—	—	6	
1870	204	12	1	—	—	8	
1880	314	23	4	—	—	11	
1890	475	39	11	—	3·8	13	
1900	701	72	21	—	7·1	16	
1910	1057	108	45	—	15·3	34	
1920	1193	158	99	1·2	24·0	64	
1930	1217	197	197	6·5	54·2	128	
1940	1363	319	292	6·9	81·8	193	
1950	1454	361	523	13·6	197·0	332	
	(million megawatt-hours electricity equivalent)						
1860	1057	15	—	—	—	6	1079
1870	1628	30	8	—	—	8	1674
1880	2511	58	43	—	—	11	2623
1890	3797	97	109	—	40	13	4056
1900	5606	179	213	—	75	16	6089
1910	8453	271	467	—	162	34	9387
1920	9540	394	1032	14	254	64	11298
1930	9735	493	2045	78	575	128	13054
1940	10904	798	3037	83	867	193	15882
1950	11632	902	5439	163	2088	332	20556

Source: O.N.U., 1956, pp. 27–8.

be obtained from atoms through the process of fusion or fission. Today this cumulative process is working faster than ever.

All these developments have brought about an extraordinary increase in the amount of energy available to man. Table 3 illustrates this development and its basic components.

The total world production of inanimate commercial energy amounted to *circa* 1·1 milliard megawatt-hours in 1860. By 1900 it had risen to *circa* 6·1 milliard and by 1950 it had reached *circa* 21 milliard. The curve indicates an overall average rate of growth of about $3\frac{1}{4}$ per cent compounded annually. There are reasons to believe that the production curve overstates the growth of energy requirements during the period 1860–1900 when there was a considerable displacement of fuel wood, etc., by commercial sources of energy. On the other hand it understates the rise in requirement during the period 1900–1950 because these years brought great increases in the efficiency of energy utilization. Actually for the half-century 1900–1950 it seems reasonable to believe that the rate of growth of world requirements of useful energy during periods free from war and depression was certainly not less than 4 per cent per year and may have reached 6 per cent per year.[1]

The growth of energy production in the long run was much greater than that of population. Thus the average world *per capita* supply increased throughout the last century. Over-all world *per capita* averages, however, mean very little. The increase in the supply of energy was by no means equally proportionate to that in population in the different parts of the world. The net result is a great inequality in world distribution of consumable energy. Table 4 illustrates this fact, showing data on *per capita* consumption of inanimate energy for selected countries. The same Table shows that there is definitely a rough correlation between *per capita* income and *per capita* consumption of inanimate energy. It is also evident that industrialized countries tend to have a *per capita* consumption of inanimate energy higher than 20 megawatt-hours (=20·000 kilowatt-hours) per year. The

1. O.N.U., 1956, pp. 11–13.

U.S. heads the list with about 62 megawatt-hours. The figure is still increasing, while more and more countries are rapidly moving in the same direction. It seems therefore reasonable to say that at an advanced stage of industrialization the *per capita* energy requirements tend to move beyond the level of 50 megawatt-hours per year.

TABLE 4. Per capita *product (1950) and consumption of energy (1952) in selected countries*

	Per capita product ($)		Energy consumption per capita (megawatt-hours)
	A	B	
U.S.A.	1810	1810	62·1
U.K.	1136	954	36·6
U.S.S.R.	1070	—	21·0
France	968	764	18·8
Italy	548	394	5·5
India	—	—	2·7

Per capita products in column A are valued by U.S.A. prices and in column B by European relative prices. Figures on energy consumption include firewood and oil shale consumption.

It is rather important to realize that high *per capita* consumption of energy not only means more energy for consumption, heating, lighting, household appliances, cars, etc., but also means more energy for production, i.e., more energy available per worker and therefore higher productivity of labour. It has also to be emphasized that the new types of energy produced have the advantage of possessing a high degree of adaptability to different uses – much more so than the energy derived from the old traditional converters.

For purely descriptive purposes, it can be useful to make a distinction between animate or physiological energy (generated in plants, animals, bacteria, molds, fungi, etc., and in its turn divided into biotic and muscular energy) and inanimate or purely physical energy (derived from wind, water, wood, peat, fossil fuels, other minerals, tidal motion, heat of the earth, radioactive elements, etc.).

From this point of view, one can say that the Industrial Revolution, by introducing large-scale exploitation of new sources of energy, dramatically changed the patterns of the energy budget of human societies. At an agricultural level any human society disposes of a very limited *per capita* supply of energy, largely physiological. At an industrial level, the energy supply is much higher and mainly inanimate. In the United States, for instance, the contribution of coal, liquid and gaseous fuels, and water-power to aggregate energy consumption passed from less than 10 per cent of the total in 1850 to more than 95 per cent around 1950.[1]

Available inanimate energy is partly derived from recurrent or inexhaustible sources, such as water-power, wind, and wood. Direct solar energy should also be included in this group (the adjective *direct* is used here because water-power, wind, and wood are in essence converted solar energy). Other inanimate energy is instead derived from irreplaceable sources, such as coal, lignite, petroleum, and natural gas.

Hitherto the Industrial Revolution has been based essentially on the exploitation of inanimate energy derived from irreplaceable sources. By 1950, more than half of the world energy income was certainly derived from irreplaceable assets.

The irreplaceable assets are coal, petroleum, natural gas, and lignite. They were formed from carbon dioxide and water in living organisms by the influence of solar radiation.

1. Schurr and Netschert, 1960, p. 36.

They are 'stored sunlight'. One can summarize the story of our happy generations in the following way: for millions and millions of years wealth was stored and cumulated. Then, someone in the family discovered the hoard – and started to dissipate it. We are now living through this fabulous dissipation. Humanity is today consuming more coal in a single year than had been generated in a hundred centuries or so during the process of carbonization.[1]

The problem arises: how long can the dissipation last? World population today is increasing faster than ever. Energy requirements are increasing at an even faster rate because of the industrialization of the underdeveloped societies and the further progress of the developed ones. The question of the 'life expectancy' of fossil fuel reserves is becoming a very pressing one. Many estimates of it have been made in recent years;[2] some are pessimistic,[3] some are optimistic.[4] Everyone admits, however, that the day will certainly come when fossil fuel reserves are exhausted.

In the long view of human history, 'man's reliance on fossil fuels for his supply of energy can be but a short episode'.[5] Figure 5 vividly illustrates this point. Proper alternative sources of energy that can substitute for fossil fuel must be found, if mankind is not to revert to an agricultural level of activity dramatically reducing not only its levels of living but also its numbers. An agricultural level of activity cannot support very much more than one milliard people on the earth. All population in excess of that number would have to disappear, in one way or another. Current scientific

1. Thirring, 1958, p. 31.
2. On the methodological problems involved in such estimates see Schurr and Netschert, 1960, p. 295.
3. Putnam, 1953.
4. Ayres and Scarlott, 1952, pp. 155–67.
5. Thirring, 1958, p. 218.

discoveries are offering more than one solution, but practical exploitation of these discoveries will largely depend on the capacity of human societies to build up the capital required for trapping economically the more 'difficult' kinds

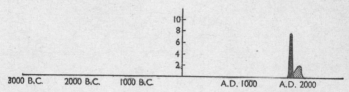

Fig. 5. Consumption of fossil fuel in historical perspective (from Thirring, 1958). The two curves are based on different estimates of future energy consumption and fossil fuel reserves

of energy. Indeed, 'it involves a great deal more work to live on income than on the accumulated capital of geological ages.'[1]

Around 1952, the annual world production of energy was in the neighbourhood of 30 thousand million megawatt-hours. Of these, only some 10 thousand millions were actually put to work. The others – two-thirds of total production – were *lost* (Table 5).

Energy can be lost in all sorts of ways. There are production and transportation losses. There are losses in the process of the interconversion of fuels. And finally there are heavy losses in the conversion of heat to mechanical energy in its application, such as the generation of unwanted heat, the evaporation of cooling water, mechanical friction, improper combustion, imperfect heat transfer, and a low load factor. As a matter of fact the largest losses occur at the consumer level where nearly half the original supply of energy is today dissipated in the form of waste heat in the course of its use.

1. Darwin, 1953, p. 75.

All this means that man is still extremely inefficient in the use of inanimate energy. In a way, we are like the first neolithic farmers. They were definitely inefficient in the use of the converters – plants and animals – that they had just learned to control. It took man thousands of years and an endless chain of discoveries to improve his efficiency in

TABLE 5. *World's energy income, 1952*

PRODUCTION	Milliards megawatt-hours electricity equivalent
coal	12·0
lignite & peat	1·3
petroleum & natural gasoline	7·7
natural gas	2·7
water power	0·4
vegetable fuels	4·6
animal energy	0·3

29·0 of which 10·4 produced in North America
5·5 „ „ W. Europe
5·0 „ „ E. Europe & U.S.S.R.

LOSSES	
in processing plants	3·6
in transmission	0·1
in use	14·0
other	1·1

18·8

PRODUCTION LESS LOSSES

10·2 of which 0·3 used in agriculture
0·8 „ „ transportation
5·8 „ „ industry
3·3 „ „ household

Source: o.n.u., 1956, pp. 3–35.

exploiting the basic discovery of the Agricultural Revolution. Similarly, a great deal of progress is still needed to reach a satisfactory degree of efficiency in the utilization of inanimate converters. The 'long march' has already begun. The steam engine of Watt had a technical efficiency below

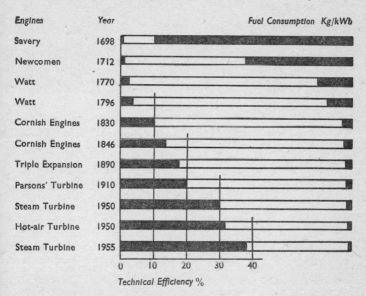

Fig. 6. The technical efficiency of steam engines, 1698–1955
(from Thirring, 1958)

5 per cent. Modern steam turbines almost reach 40 per cent (Fig. 6). The average technical efficiency of thermo-electric power stations passed from less than 9 per cent around 1920 to *circa* 24 per cent in 1952. Considering an economy as a whole, the U.S. between 1920 and 1955 experienced a decline in the input of energy relative to Gross National Product on the order of 35 per cent: in other words, because of

improvements in the over-all productive efficiency of the economy, increases in the thermal efficiency of energy use, and the growth of electrification, in 1955 the U.S. could produce the same quantity of goods and services with 35 per cent less energy than in 1920.[1]

These are indeed remarkable improvements. But there is still a long way to go.

1. Schurr and Netschert, 1960, pp. 16–17.

CHAPTER 3

Production and Consumption

MAN needs capital to trap energy. And still more capital to exploit obtained energy for productive purposes. Capital accumulation is a necessary condition for any society's survival and progress. And, conversely, any society's survival and progress is in a way a measure of that society's capacity to accumulate capital and use it efficiently.

There is definitely a correlation between capital and output. In a hunting economy, the capital needs are very limited: a few bones – used as tools or as weapons – and (in more developed cultures) bows, arrows, and stone implements. In an agricultural economy the capital needed is of quite a different quality and magnitude: stocks of seeds, fertilizers, ploughs and other implements, draught animals, silos, mills, boats, wagons, and so forth. In an industrial economy, capital needs are still more complex and much larger: machinery, railways, chemical and atomic plants, dams, research laboratories, and so forth. The greater the production, the greater the volume of capital needed. On the other hand, it is also true that the greater the production, the greater the possibility of capital formation.

We do not possess enough information about the patterns of production, consumption, and capital formation in a hunting economy. In this chapter we will limit our analysis to the patterns generally prevailing in agricultural and industrial societies.

THE AGRICULTURAL SOCIETY

Capital is made possible by saving. Only by forgoing present consumption can a society shift resources to the production of capital equipment. It is generally admitted that in any agricultural society, given the low *per capita* income, *per capita* saving is – in absolute terms – very low. This circumstance is further aggravated by the way saved resources are used. Temples, pyramids, mansions, jewellery, warfare, and so forth generally absorb a large quota of resources squeezed out of current private saving. Furthermore, pre-industrial societies are typically characterized by inadequate transport facilities. Mass transportation is generally non-existent and all communications are costly and insecure. Consequently any pre-industrial society must keep inventories in much larger proportion to current production than any industrial society does. This is true for any type of commodity, but particularly so for basic necessities. 'Keeping capital intact' recurrently requires large quotas of saving to rebuild inventories depleted by frequent famines. Such inventories are a form of investment, i.e. of capital accumulation, but with a 'stabilizing' character. Generally investment of a 'developmental' character is very small in any agricultural society.

It has been indicated that a society needs different amounts of capital at different stages. In order to pass from, let us say, an agricultural type of economic organization to an industrial one, a society must make substantial efforts to build up the capital necessary for the transition. If this transition is gradual, the process can be relatively smooth. If, on the contrary, the transition is forced to take place in a very short time, the process is bound to be painful. In such case, 'industrial' capital must be squeezed out from an income that is still 'agricultural'. The more abrupt the transition, the greater the hardships.

To accomplish the transition, a given society must reach an absolute level of capital formation – the so-called 'critical minimum level', failing which the transition is not possible.[1] But an agricultural society cannot industrialize by increasing beyond the 'critical minimum' the total volume of wooden ploughs or hoe-sticks produced, any more than hunters can become farmers by increasing their output of flaked stones and arrows. Indeed, the required changes in capital formation are of qualitative as well as of a quantatitive nature. The qualitative changes imply that the active population must acquire new skills, and the total population must adopt new patterns of living. This problem will be discussed later in Chapter 6. Here we only have to remember that the need for new skills may mean that further capital is needed for investment in education.

In all agricultural societies of our past we find that, mainly because of limitations of energy sources known and exploited, the great mass of people can hardly afford to satisfy anything but the more elementary needs – food, clothing, and housing, and even these at rather unsatisfactory levels. Correspondingly, most of the available resources are employed in agriculture, textile manufacture, and building.

Of these three sectors, agriculture is always by far the predominant one. It absorbs the greatest quota of available capital and labour. Further, it somehow represents the pivotal point around which all other activities tend to revolve. Building makes a large use of timber. And textile

1. Liebenstein, 1957, Chapter 8.

manufacture uses materials – woollen or linen, cotton or silk – that are also produced 'in the fields'.

On the fringe, there is always some trade – in one form or another – heavily concentrated on agricultural products (grains, wines, spices, timber, etc.) and textiles. In terms of labour employed, trade is generally a minor sector, and merchants a minority. But trade always plays a strategically dynamic role. It allows specialization and better use of available resources. Its fluctuations are of paramount importance to the fortunes of the whole country. All historical records seem to demonstrate that where trade flourished, demographic and economic levels were the highest attainable within the range of agricultural possibilities. Actually, almost all the great agricultural civilizations of the pre-industrial past were founded on the expansion of the mercantile sector. And it was an exaggerated expansion of this sector in seventeenth- and eighteenth-century England that created the material preconditions for the emergence of the Industrial Revolution.

THE INDUSTRIAL SOCIETY

Thanks to the exploitation of new sources of energy, larger amounts of capital, and more efficient use of factors of production, *per capita* real income is vastly greater in any industrial society than in any agricultural society. Consequently, the quality of the diet of the mass of people is generally better. Improvements are also generally experienced in clothing and housing. New and 'higher' human needs are satisfied on a mass scale. Actually, expenditure on such 'higher' items as transportation, medical care, education, amusements, etc., increases more than proportionately.

Thus, expenditure on food – although increasing in absolute terms – decreases as a percentage of total private expenditure.

In connexion with the exploitation of new kinds of energy and new prevailing consumption patterns, one observes a general decline in the relative importance of agriculture among the various productive sectors while other productive sectors tend to lose their dependence on agriculture. The building industry substitutes steel and cement for timber. The textile industry substitutes artificial fibres (rayon, dacron, etc.) for natural ones. The pharmaceutical industry substitutes chemical products for spices and herbs. Even the food industry follows the trend: vitamin pills tend to replace natural fruits, and Coca Cola tends to replace wine. It has been said that before the Industrial Revolution of all the things man used nearly eighty per cent were derived from the plant and animal kingdom, with only about twenty per cent from the mineral kingdom.[1] These proportions cannot be accepted at their face value. But they can undoubtedly be taken as a gross approximation. With the Industrial Revolution the situation they describe is being substantially reversed. Correspondingly, both the percentage of total active population employed in agriculture and the proportion of income produced by the agricultural sector shrink markedly while a great expansion is generally experienced in the new key sectors: the chemical, the metallurgical, and the mechanical.

Statistical material available on the economic development of Europe and the United States during the last hundred years vividly illustrates some of the patterns sketched briefly in the previous paragraphs.

1. Mather, 1944, pp. 55–6.

Labour increased because of population growth (see Chapter 5). It also became proportionately more and more absorbed by the secondary and tertiary sectors at the expense of agriculture. Data on this trend have already been presented in Chapter 1 (Tables 1 and 2), pp. 27 and 30. The absolute volume of capital formation also increased remarkably in the long run, and proportionately it took more and more the form of machinery and producer durable equipment at the expense of construction and inventories. In the United States during the period 1869–98, construction absorbed about 70 per cent of net capital formation, net addition to inventories about 18 per cent, and producer durable equipment about 14 per cent (with about minus 3 per cent as net change in claims against foreign countries). During the period 1909–38 construction shrank to less than 50 per cent, net addition to inventories diminished to about 12 per cent, and producer durable equipment increased to 22 per cent (with about plus 17 per cent as net change in claims against foreign countries).[1]

The growth of inputs (labour and capital) and their progressively more efficient utilization brought forward an extraordinary long expansion of production. Population increased. But production increased noticeably faster than population. And *per capita* income improved remarkably over the long run.

Tables 7 and 8 summarize the growth of population, national product, and national product *per capita* during the last century in selected countries. Table 9 shows how the importance of the agricultural sector in the formation of aggregate income diminished everywhere.

The key role in all this development was played by the industrial sector.

1. Kuznetz, 1946, p. 55, and Kuznetz, 1952.

TABLE 6. *The national income of the United States of America, 1800–1948*

	Population (millions)	Net national income ($ milliards) 1929 prices	Net national income *per capita* ($) 1929 prices	Net capital formation as percentage of net national product at constant (1929) prices	Percentage of gainfully occupied population employed in agriculture	Per cent share of agriculture in national income at constant prices
1799–1800	5·3	—	—	—	73	39
1869–78	43·5	9·4	216	14·3	50	27
1879–88	54·9	17·9	326	14·6	46	21
1889–98	67·6	24·2	358	16·3	40	19
1899–1908	81·3	37·5	461	13·9	34	16
1909–18	97·6	50·3	515	12·5	29	13
1919–28	112·9	69·0	612	10·6	24	11
1929–38	126·0	72·0	572	1·7	20	10
1939–48	137·8	108·9	790	7·9	13	8

Source: Kuznetz, 1952.

TABLE 7. *Population and net national income in selected countries mid nineteenth to mid twentieth century*

	Period considered	Population (millions)	Monetary unit used	Net national product (milliards)
United States	1869–78	44·6	1929 $	10
	1950– 4	157·5	,,	143
United Kingdom	1860– 9	25·8	1912–13 pounds	788
	1949–53	50·4	,,	4254
France				
(excluding Alsace-Lorraine)	1861–70	37·9	1938 francs	136
(including Alsace-Lorraine)	1949–53	42·2	,,	409
Germany				
(territory before 1913)	1860– 9	39·2	1928 marks	18
(Western Republic)	1950– 4	48·6	,,	69
Italy	1862– 8	26·7	1938 lire	41
	1950– 3	47·8	,,	174
Russia				
(European)	1870	64·0	1900 roubles	3
(Interwar Territory)	1954	213·0	,,	36
Japan	1878–87	37·2	1928–32 yen	2
	1950– 4	85·5	,,	19

Source: Kuznetz, 1956, pp. 53–90.

66

TABLE 8. *Rates of growth of population, national product, and product* per capita *at constant prices in selected countries from the mid nineteenth to mid twentieth century*

	Initial period	Terminal period	Population	National product	National product *per capita*
				Per cent average change per year	
United Kingdom	1860– 9	1949–53	0·8	2·2	1·3
France	1841–50	1949–53	0·1	1·5	1·4
Germany	1860– 9	1950– 4	1·0	2·7	1·5
Sweden	1861– 8	1950– 4	0·7	3·6	2·8
Italy	1862– 8	1950– 4	0·7	1·8	1·0
Russia & U.S.S.R.	1870	1954	1·3	3·1	1·5
United States	1869–78	1950– 4	1·7	4·1	2·0
Canada	1870– 9	1950– 4	1·8	4·1	1·9
Japan	1878–87	1950– 4	1·3	4·2	2·6
Australia	1898–1903	1950–	41·7	2·8	1·0

Source: Kuznetz, 1959, pp. 20–1.

TABLE 9. *Percentage share of agriculture in national income of selected countries*

	about 1770	about 1870	about 1950
France		45	16
Germany		30	15
Great Britain	45	15	4
Italy		57	29
Japan		63	23
Sweden		43	14
United States		30	5
U.S.S.R.		55	22

The index of world industrial production since 1870 has progressed as follows: [1]

1870:	100	1932:	540
1900:	310	1937:	950
1913:	530	1946:	1000
1920:	500	1952:	1710
1929:	800		

Detailed statistics available for Western Europe and the United States since the beginning of the twentieth century allow for these areas a detailed analysis of the patterns of industrial development. Between 1901 and 1955 the volume of 'industrial production' [2] increased in the United States at an average of 3·7 per cent per year; industrial product per head at an average of 2·4 per cent per year. In Western Europe,[3] the volume of 'industrial production' [4] increased at an average of 2·3 per cent per year, and industrial product per head at an average of 1·6 per cent per year.

A good deal of the increase in production was due to the increase in total factor productivity. In the United States productivity gains in manufacturing and mining averaged during the period 1899–1953 a rate of 2 per cent per year (against a rate of less than 1 per cent in agriculture).[5]

1. O.N.U., 1956, p. 13.
2. 'Industrial production' is here defined as production resulting from mining, quarrying, and manufacturing.
3. For the definition of Western Europe as referred to in this chapter see Table 10.
4. 'Industrial production' is here defined as for the United States (see footnote 2) with the addition of the production of electricity and gas.
5. Kendrick, 1956, pp. 9–10. Output per unit of labour input showed actually an average rate of increase of 2·4 per cent per year while output per unit of capital input showed an average rate of

TABLE 10. *Growth of industrial production in Western Europe and United States, 1901–55*

	Population (millions)		General index industrial production (volume) 1938 = 100		Index industrial production per head (W.E. 1955 = 100)	
	W.E.	U.S.	W.E.	U.S.	W.E.	U.S.
1901	195·0	77·6	44	35	37	74
1913	216·6	97·2	69	66	51	109
1929	234·0	121·8	86	124	60	165
1937	245·7	129·0	102	127	67	160
1955	284·1	165·2	177	291	100	285

W.E. = Western Europe = O.E.E.C. Member Countries (Austria, Belgium, Denmark, France, Germany, Greece, Ireland, Italy, Luxemburg, Netherlands, Norway, Saar, Sweden, Turkey, United Kingdom).

Source: Paretti and Bloch, 1956, Tables 2, 28, and 30.

INDUSTRIAL PRODUCTION ANALYSED

The overall growth of industrial production both in Europe and the United States was accompanied by a marked shift in the relative importance of the various sectors of industrial manufacture. We have already referred to this phenomenon and its causes in the previous paragraphs. Let us assess some of its quantitative aspects. At the beginning of the twentieth century, food and textiles together covered in Western Europe 47 per cent of total manufacturing production and

---

increase of 1·3 per cent. This means that capital increased per unit of labour input *circa* 0·8 per cent per year in the economy as a whole. Since output per unit of capital has generally risen over the period despite the greater increase in capital than in labour inputs, one has to admit that innovation has been on the whole capital-saving as well as labour-saving. For comparisons with other countries see Tinbergen, 1942; Aukrust, 1959.

44 per cent in the United States. By 1955 the two sectors represented only 21 per cent in Western Europe and 19 per cent in the United States.

During the same period the share of metal products increased from 16 to 34 per cent in Western Europe and from 10 to 41 per cent in the United States. Chemicals similarly passed from 5 to 14 per cent in Western Europe and from 5 to 13 per cent in the United States. Altogether the metal products and chemicals sectors currently account for 48 per cent of total manufacturing production in Western Europe and 54 per cent in the United States.

The expansion of *per capita* real income allowed drastic improvements in the levels of living and the satisfaction of other than elementary needs on a mass scale. The following indicators may be used to demonstrate the levels of economic welfare. Three-quarters of mankind are still tied – and to exceed: [1]

Energy consumed *per capita* per year (megawatt-hours)	over	20
Annual freight carried *per capita* (ton-miles)	over	1500
Per cent illiterate (population age ten and over)	below	5
Elementary school teachers per 1000 population	over	5
Doctors per 1000 population	over	1
Expectation of life at birth (years)	over	60
All foods: calories *per capita* per day	over	2500
Animal proteins: oz. *per capita* per day	over	1·5
Fats: oz. *per capita* per day	over	4
Percentage of calories of animal origin	over	20
Expenditure on food and drink as percentage of total private expenditure	below	35

Today only a small minority enjoys these levels of economic welfare. Three-quarters of mankind are still tied to agricultural levels of living. Undergoing the Industrial

1. Bennett, 1951, pp. 632–49; Spengler, 1956, p. 334.

TABLE 11. *Composition of industrial production in Western Europe and United States by major sectors, 1901–55*

	Western Europe						United States				
	1901	1913	1929	1937	1955		1899	1914	1929	1937	1955
Total manufacturing	100	100	100	100	100		100	100	100	100	100
Food	27	19	16	15	13		24	20	14	15	11
Textiles	20	18	14	12	8		20	19	11	12	8
Basic metals	7	10	10	10	9		9	10	10	9	9
Metal products	16	24	27	28	34		10	13	33	31	41
Chemicals	5	6	10	10	14		5	6	8	10	13
Others	25	24	23	25	22		32	32	24	23	18

Source: Paretti and Bloch, 1956, Table 18. For the definition of 'Western Europe' as referred to in this table see Table 10.

71

TABLE 12. *Per cent composition of private consumption in the United States and in the United Kingdom, 1950*

	U.S.	U.K.
Food	22·1	31·3
Alcoholic beverages	1·4	2·0
Tobacco	1·5	1·7
Clothing and household textiles	13·7	12·7
Housing	3·7	5·9
Fuel, light, and water	6·4	7·6
Household goods	15·4	10·0
Household and personal services	2·6	4·4
Transport equipment and services	15·2	5·0
Communication services	1·1	0·7
Recreation and entertainment	5·4	9·4
Health	3·4	4·2
Education	2·6	3·3
Miscellaneous	5·5	1·8
	100·0	100·0

Source: Gilbert, 1958, p. 60.

Revolution is their great hope, but one of the biggest among the many difficulties that these underdeveloped masses have to overcome is the fact that they are multiplying themselves at an appalling rate. It is at this point that we have to turn our attention to the population problem.

CHAPTER 4

Births and Deaths

PRIMITIVE SOCIETY

PRIMITIVE hunters and food-gatherers – whether pre-historic men, modern Australian aborigines, or contemporary Eskimos – are always scant in numbers and extremely scattered. Anthropological and archaeological research confirms this proposition. The general consensus is that density among hunting and food-gathering peoples is far too great if it is as much as one person per square kilometer or some 2·5 per square mile.[1] Probably only a few fishing groups very favourably situated have experienced higher densities. In fact, actual densities varied extremely, not only with area but also with climatic change, the diffusion or disappearance of game, and the growth and decline of various cultures. The density values that one can find for various societies are so vastly different that any average would be meaningless. But the highest densities are so low that they are more significant than any possible average.

Some time ago the belief was common that early man's fecundity was lower than that of civilized man, and that this was the main cause for the small size of Paleolithic societies. Today this theory has been generally abandoned. We do not possess reliable figures, but indirect evidence supports the view that the Paleolithic populations had very high mortality rates. Since the species survived, we must admit that primitive man also had a very high fertility rate.[2]

1. See Ratzel, 1891, Part II, pp. 255–64; Forde, 1955, p. 376; Krzywicki, 1934, pp. 52–8; Braidwood and Reed, 1957, pp. 21–3.
2. Wolfe, 1933, pp. 35–60.

The high birth- and death-rates were associated with a short average length of life. Here again we run into the difficulty of extremely poor information and we can express our concept only in rough quantitative terms. By analysing fossil remains of 187 Europeans of the Neanderthal group, Vallois was able to ascertain that 'more than a third died before reaching the age of 20, and the great majority of the rest died between the age of 20 and the age of 40. Beyond this limit, there are only 16 individuals, most of whom certainly died between the age of 40 and the age of 50.'[1] Weidenreich, analysing the fossil remains of 38 individuals of the Asiatic Sinanthropus population (a much earlier group than the Neanderthal) substantially confirmed the results of Vallois. Out of the 38 Sinanthropi it was possible to assess probable age at death for 22. Of these, it seems that 15 died when less than 14 years old, 3 died between the ages of 15 and 29, 3 between 40 and 50, and only one seems to have survived beyond 50.[2] Evidence collected for hunting-stage societies of historic times generally agrees with these findings. The age of fifty was rarely attained and 'the centre of gravity of these societies moves towards the lower age-groups.'[3]

In regard to causes of death, Weidenreich observed that most of the fossil remains of prehistoric man clearly indicate a violent death.[4] For Paleolithic man of historic time, Krzywicki arrived at a similar conclusion, observing that the most frequent causes of death were infanticide, war, and headhunting.[5] The low density of population was in a way a protection against epidemics. It is indeed difficult to see how, with sparse populations organized into small bands

1. Vallois, 1937, p. 525.   2. Weidenreich, 1949, pp. 194–5.
3. Krzywicki, 1934, pp. 243–54.   4. Weidenreich, 1949, p. 196.
5. Krzywicki, 1934, pp. 101–14.

wandering over limited territories, contagious diseases can have had the importance that they have assumed under other demographic conditions.[1] But it is not difficult to believe that illness and starvation must have taken on the whole a heavy toll of human life in Paleolithic and Mesolithic societies,[2] especially among infants.

AGRICULTURAL SOCIETIES

Agricultural societies began very early to be interested in the numbers of their members, either for military or fiscal reasons. Through interpretation of surviving records and with the assistance of archaeological evidence it is not impossible to reach rough estimates of population totals and densities for ancient societies. On both fertility and mortality, however, there is no information available until a very late period. Records for some areas of Europe start in the late sixteenth century, but this is exceptional. Generally, available records start much later. The careful collection of detailed statistics requires a quantitatively orientated culture and organizational capacities that – apart from a few exceptions – are not characteristic of agricultural or pastoral societies. The evidence that can be derived from funerary inscriptions hardly allows any meaningful conclusion in regard to the average length of life.[3]

1. Bates, 1953, p. 707; Hare, 1954, pp. 35–47.
2. In regard to illness, one has to admit that all available evidence seems to indicate that primitive man was more resistant to noxious infections by bacteria than is true today. See Weidenreich, 1949, p. 203.
3. See the works quoted on p. 78, footnote 2. On the great difficulties of estimating the average length of life on the basis of funerary inscriptions see Henry, 1957, pp. 149–52, and Henry, 1959, pp. 327–9.

However poor, the material available suggests that any agricultural society – whether sixteenth-century Italy, seventeenth century France, or nineteenth-century India – tends to adhere to a definite set of patterns in the structure and movements of birth- and death-rates. Crude birth-rates are very high throughout, ranging between 35 and 50 per thousand. Within such range, the actual value of the birth-rate in any given agricultural society varies according to numerous factors: age and sex composition of the population, sanitary and economic conditions, short-run factors such as wars, epidemics, famines, or prosperity, and long-run socio-cultural factors. Among these one might recall the very attitude toward marriage (India for instance has always been a country of universal marriage where, in most instances, a girl is married before reaching puberty and where practically every woman is married by twenty; preindustrial Europe, on the contrary, has always attached great value to the unmarried status and the proportion of unmarried people has generally been relatively high), the tendency to marry at one age rather than another, the attitudes toward birth-control, etc. Death-rates are also very high, but *normally* lower than the birth-rates – ranging generally between 30 and 40 per thousand.

The population of an agricultural society is characterized by a normal rate of growth of 0·5 to 1·0 per cent per year. To give a meaning to this figure I can quote an exercise in astronomical arithmetic by P. C. Putnam: if the race had sprung from a couple living not long before agriculture was discovered – let us say 10,000 B.C. – and if its members had expanded at the rate of one per cent per year since then, the world population would form today a sphere of living flesh many thousand light years in diameter, and expanding with a radial velocity that, neglecting relativity, would be many times faster than light.[1] This has not happened because throughout the demographic history of agricultural societies, death-rates show a remarkable tendency to recurrent, sudden dramatic peaks that reach levels as high as 150 or 300 or even 500 per thousand. On a few occasions these peaks coincided with wars. But much more frequently they were the result of epidemics and famines that wiped out a good part of the existing population. Reference is often made to the famous Black Death as if it were an exceptional disaster. Admittedly this unfortunate case deserves some special mention, for all Europe was then struck more or less at the same time. But one has to remember that the sudden disappearance of a fifth of the population or a third or even half, was, every once in a while, a recurrent catastrophe of local experience. The statistics collected by Father Mols for medieval Europe offer eloquent evidence of these disasters.[2] The intensity and frequency of the peaks controlled the size of agricultural societies.

A highly-fluctuating death-rate is an index of inadequate control over environment.[3] The demographic density of most agricultural societies was out of proportion to their technical capacity to control crop fluctuations and their consequences as well as epidemic diseases. Whenever a given agricultural population grew beyond a given 'ceiling', the probability increased of some sudden catastrophe that would drastically reduce the population itself

In normal times, a large proportion of the deaths were represented by infant mortality. Of 1000 newborn children, 200 to 500 usually died within a year. Many of the remaining ones died before reaching the age of seven. A famous

1. Putnam, 1950, p. 18.
2. Mols, 1955, Vol. 2, pp. 425–84.
3. Gosh, 1946, pp. 62–3.

TABLE 13. *Crude birth- and death-rates (per thousand) in selected countries, 1750–1950*

	Birth-rates					Death-rates				
	1751 1755	1801 1805	1851 1855	1905 1909	1950	1751 1755	1801 1805	1851 1855	1905 1909	1950
AFRICA										
Egypt				45·2	44·4				26·5	19·1
Un. of South Africa (White pop.)					25·1					8·7
AMERICA										
Canada					27·1					9·0
Mexico				30·0	45·5					16·2
United States					23·5				15·4	9·6
Argentina					25·5					9·0
Brazil					43·0					19·0
Chile				38·8	34·0				32·5	15·0
Venezuela					42·6					10·9
ASIA										
China					45·0					25·0
India				48·0	24·9				43·0	16·1
Pakistan					19·0					12·2
Japan				31·9	28·2				20·9	10·9

EUROPE

	1	2	3	4	5	6	7	8	9	10
Austria	35·0							15·6		12·4
Belgium		34·0		25·1				16·9		12·5
Denmark				28·4				18·6		9·2
England & Wales			33·9	26·7	30·0	23·0	22·7	15·9	16·2	11·6
United Kingdom								16·3	14·1	11·7
Finland	45·3	38·4	36·3	31·0	28·6	24·7	28·2	24·5	15·1	10·1
France	35·0	31·7	26·1	20·1		26·3	24·1	20·6	17·7	12·7
Germany			34·6	32·3			27·2	16·2	19·5	10·3
Greece				33·6				20·0	18·3	7·1
Netherlands				30·0				22·7	20·3	7·5
Hungary				36·3				21·0	14·7	11·5
Ireland				23·4				21·3	25·7	12·7
Italy				32·6				19·5	17·2	9·8
Norway	34·4	28·2	32·5	26·7	25·0	24·1	17·3	19·4	14·1	9·1
Portugal				33·5				24·4	21·6	12·2
Spain				33·7				20·3	24·5	10·9
Sweden	37·1	31·4	31·8	25·6	26·3	24·4	21·7	16·4	14·6	10·0
Switzerland			29·0	26·4			23·6	18·2	16·5	10·1
Yugoslavia								30·3		13·0
U.S.S.R.	48·0		48·0	45·5			40·0	26·5	29·4	9·6

sixteenth-century physician, Jerome Cardano of Pavia, used to maintain that he could cure anyone on condition that the patient was not younger than seven or older than seventy.[1]

The high toll of infants and youth drastically cut down the average length of life. All available information for numerous societies seems to indicate that the 'agricultural' life expectancy at birth generally averages twenty to thirty-five years.[2] Also those who reach the age of five have little chance of surviving beyond fifty.[3]

THE INDUSTRIAL REVOLUTION

The Industrial Revolution changes the general picture drastically again.

Hitherto, all societies that have been industrialized seem to have experienced an almost total disappearance of the recurrent peaks of the death rate. The reasons are manifold. New scientific knowledge about plants and livestock, extraordinary improvements in transportation, progress in medicine and sanitation – all have allowed men to cope with famines and epidemic diseases. Two of the three main causes of the peaks have definitely been brought under control. Unfortunately, one cannot say the same of the third cause, war.

1. Aleati, 1957, pp. 95–6.
2. Dublin, Lotka, and Spiegelman, 1949, pp. 28–43; Stolnitz, 1954–5, pp. 27–8; Burn, 1953, pp. 1–31; Bellido, 1955, pp. 117–23; Russell, 1958, pp. 22–32.
3. In comparing these figures with those quoted for the hunting stage, one should remember that remains of adult people have mainly been preserved from Paleolithic times. An average age at death calculated on the basis of the data collected by Vallois or Weidenreich would therefore tend to ignore mortality in the very young children.

TABLE 14. *Infant mortality (total infant deaths per thousand live births) in selected countries, 1900–50*

	1900	1950
Sweden	96	22
Low Countries	147	26
Norway	88	27
Denmark	126	32
Switzerland	139	32
Great Britain	145	33
Finland	135	42
France	149	53
Belgium	153	53
Ireland	102	47
Germany	207	55
Austria	221	66
Italy	168	68
Spain	195	69
Western Europe (average)	148	45
New Zealand		23
Australia		24
United States	162	33
Canada		41
Japan		60
U.S.S.R.		81
Mexico		96
India		137
Chile		153

Source: Data for Europe are derived from Chasteland, 1960, p. 68. For non-European countries data are derived from Febvay and Croze, 1954, p. 390. For U.S.S.R., Kantner, 1960, p. 40. For the U.S.A., U.S. Bureau of Census 1960, p. 28.

The technical progress that has enabled man to control famines and epidemics, has increased his destructive efficiency in warfare. This is not the proper place to speculate about the future. But one cannot help thinking that unless industrial societies learn to control war (and for the moment there is no evidence that they are moving in this direction) they may again experience demographic catastrophes – possibly of suicidal magnitude.

The Industrial Revolution also made gains possible in regard to what Sauvy calls 'normal death',[1] i.e. the death-rate in normal times. Progress in medicine and sanitation, better nutrition, and higher levels of living have practically eliminated many diseases and reduced the incidence of many others. The 'normal' death-rate has been pushed down, and in industrial societies it tends to be below 15 per thousand (Table 13).

The most important component in the fall of the death-rate has generally been a drastic reduction in infant mortality. Today in industrial societies, infant deaths tend to be less than 50 per thousand live births (Table 14). This, together with the control gained over many diseases and better levels of living, has noticeably increased the average length of life. In industrial societies life expectation at birth tends to be over 60.[2]

We will discuss later the behaviour of the birth-rate under the impact of the Industrial Revolution. Let us just note here that in any industrial society it tends to range below 25 per thousand (Table 13).

LEVELLING UP THE BIRTH- AND DEATH-RATES

The preceding observations seem to suggest that for any one of the three basic types of economic organization there exists

1. Sauvy, 1958, pp. 31–70.
2. Stolnitz, 1954–5; Chasteland, 1960, pp. 59–88. See also Table 15.

– at least potentially – an equilibrium mechanism that controls population growth. For the hunting-fishing societies we suppose – rather vaguely, with allowance made for some taboo contraceptive practices and counting infanticide in the death-rate – that the equilibrium mechanism consisted of a high death-rate matching a high birth-rate. How fluctuating these rates could have been we simply do not know. For the agricultural societies we can state more precisely that the mechanism generally consisted of a high and highly fluctuating death-rate that checked a high but more stable birth-rate: the death rate was normally lower than the birth-rate and the population tended to increase, but eventually an abnormal peak of the death-rate wiped out the 'surplus' population. Then the cycle started again. For industrial societies it seems that the mechanism should mainly consist in adjustment of the birth-rate to a very low death-rate. The looser the adjustment of the birth-rate to the death-rate, the higher the probability of the re-appearance of the peaks as equilibrating devices.[1]

TABLE 15. *Expectation of life at birth and at sixty in Western Europe, 1900–50*

	1900	1950
at birth	47	67
at sixty	14	17

Source: Chasteland, 1960, p. 71. The countries considered are Sweden, Denmark, Norway, The Low Countries, Switzerland, Ireland, Belgium, Great Britain, France, Finland, Germany, Italy, Austria, Spain.

1. There is a long-run incompatibility of noticeably divergent fertility-rates and death-rates. The reason lies in the absurdity of continued geometric increase. The consequences of such an increase in the long run is a population incompatible with any estimated resources, no matter how large the estimate. See Coale, 1959, p. 36, and also later on in this book, Chapter 5, p. 101, footnote 1.

These mechanisms [1] have never been so rigid as to stabilize any population completely. At any stage, both birth- and death-rates have a range of possible variation. Furthermore, and particularly in regard to agricultural societies, periods of peace and prosperity tend to slow the frequency of abnormal peaks in the death-rate while periods of war and disorder tend to increase it. These circumstances allow for massive population movements either up or down. The secular demographic 'cycles' of China before the nineteenth century [2] or the '*grosse Wellen*' of the German population [3] are typical examples of this kind of movement.

If it is true that the equilibrium mechanisms are flexible enough to allow substantial growth or decline in a population, it is also true that the very existence of an equilibrium mechanism somehow conditions and limits the possible range of movement. Further, movements inside the limits allowed by the equilibrating mechanism are generally the product of particular local cultural or political development and are therefore geographically limited.

The 'demographic explosions' that accompanied both the Agricultural and Industrial Revolutions show, on the con-

1. The term equilibrium is here used to mean not absolute stability, but rather the lack of any substantial and sustained movement of growth or decline. 'Natural populations tend to fluctuate about some equilibrium figure. This fact has long been recognized by biologists. . . . From a short-term point of view, populations are in only approximate equilibriums, but viewed from the time of scale of the Pleistocene, slowly expanding populations of man can be considered as being essentially in equilibrium' (Bartholomew and Birdsell, 1953, p. 494).

2. Ta Chen, 1946, pp. 4–6.

3. Mackenroth, 1953, pp. 112–19.

trary, very different characteristics. First of all, as they follow the diffusion of the Revolution, they become world wide. Secondly, they tend to be of exceptional intensity and magnitude. It seems really as if, during each Revolution, the population is 'getting out of control'. And, in fact, one way of viewing these explosions is to consider them as the result of the disruption of a prevailing equilibrium mechanism.

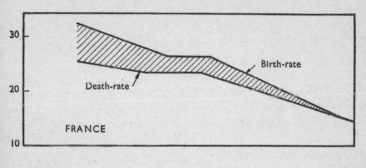

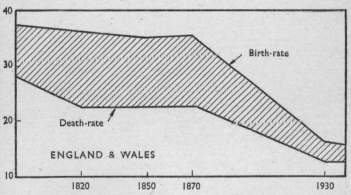

Fig. 7. Diagram showing the movements of the crude birth- and death-rates in England and France, 1750–1950

The span of time before a new equilibrium replaces the disrupted one is the period during which the population 'gets out of control' and explodes.

We do not have enough information about the first of the two Revolutions to be able to detect how and why one equilibrium was broken and a new one came to replace it. But we are pretty well informed on the explosive mechanism of the second Revolution. Here, the general patterns are as follows. The starting point (equilibrium of the agricultural stage) is a high birth-rate (35–55 per thousand) and a high (normally 30–40 per thousand) and highly fluctuating (up to 150–300–500 per thousand) death-rate. With the Industrial Revolution the high, recurrent death peaks tend to disappear. This fact by itself is bound to start an explosive growth, because the normal death-rate is from the very beginning lower than the prevailing birth-rate and the abnormal peaks of the death-rate were a vital element in the former equilibrium mechanism.[1] However, this is not the entire story. Under the impact of progress in medicine and sanitation, and improvement in the diet of the

1. Helleiner, 1957. A good illustration is offered by contemporary India. Between 1891 and 1921 a high and nearly constant level of fertility was combined with relatively high but fluctuating death-rates. Death-rates fluctuated in response to famines induced by crop failures and to the incidence of major epidemics. The result was a very slight rise in population. Over the interval 1891 to 1921 the total growth was little more than 5 per cent, or an average of less than one-sixth of one per cent per annum. After 1921, while the level of fertility and that of 'normal' death remained constant, the sudden and violent peaks of the death-rate due to epidemics and famines disappeared. The absence of major calamities of this sort since 1921 has produced a growth rate that over the period 1921–51 has exceeded one per cent per annum. Coale and Hoover, 1958, pp. 29, 31, and 54. Similar remarks can also be made for the growth of Italian population from 1650 to 1850.

people, the 'normal' death-rate also undergoes a downward movement. The birth-rate too eventually should follow a downward course. But the movements of *this* rate are subject to a complex interplay of heterogeneous forces. Davis and Blake have indicated eleven 'intermediate variables' that influence fertility. And they have found that no culture has ever been able to acquire low fertility-values for *all* of them.[1] Under the pressure of numerous and different cultural, institutional, and economic forces, the birth-rate is bound to show a certain degree of resistance. It adjusts to the pull of the death-rate with a time lag. The extent of this time lag may be negligible or considerable.[2] France and England (with Wales) offer good examples of different forms of development (see Fig. 7). In both cases the disappearance of the death peaks, leaving an uncontrolled gap between the birth- and death-rates, produced a demographic explosion. However, while in France the birth-rate quickly followed the death-rate, in England and Wales the birth-rate responded to the pull with a noticeable lag and up to 1820 the gap increased considerably, adding new fuel to the explosive growth.

We have been dealing explicitly with societies that have been industrialized. Yet, today, we witness a new, interesting development. Industrialized societies, having acquired the technical capacity to control disease, felt and still feel a humanitarian urge to give medical assistance to societies

1. Davis and Blake, 1956, pp. 211–35. See also U.N., 1958.
2. In some cases because the lag can be further aggravated by the fact that at the very beginning of the process the birth-rate not only does not respond to the 'pull' of the death-rate, but actually tends to move – though only for a short time – in the opposite direction. This can be due for instance to a lowering of the average age of marriage.

that basically are still agricultural. The consequences of such action are appalling. 'In Europe knowledge of death control was slowly developed and growth of population was therefore gradual. In the underdeveloped countries the accumulated knowledge of two centuries is immediately available and death-rates have therefore fallen much faster than they ever did in Western Europe. In Ceylon, to quote an extreme but illuminating case, the malarial mosquito has been wiped out by DDT and deaths fell from 22 to 12 per thousand in the seven years from 1945 to 1952 (immediately after spraying with DDT the death-rate fell from 20 to 14 per thousand in the single year 1946–7), a fall which took seventy years in England and Wales. In Mauritius a fall from 27 to 15 death per thousand, which took 100 years to achieve in England and Wales, also came about in seven years.'[1] The suddenness of the fall of the death-rate,[2] combined with the fact that some of the 'underdeveloped' countries are not prepared for the cultural changes that the Industrial Revolution implies (especially in regard to birth-control), causes a dramatic enlargement of the 'demographic gap.' Again to take Ceylon as an example, the precipitous decline in mortality was not accompanied by any measurable changes in fertility: the crude birth-rate has remained over 40 per thousand.[3] With an 'agricultural' birth-rate and an 'industrial' death-rate, the demographic explosion is bound to assume alarming proportions. In Ceylon the annual rate of natural growth was 4·6 per thousand in the period 1871–80, 9·3 in 1901–10, 13·4 in 1931–40, 17·1 in

1. P.E.P., 1956, p. 12.
2. Further information on the fall of the death-rate in Davis, 1956, pp. 305–18.
3. Taeuber, 1956, p. 757; Sarkan, 1957.

1941–5, 25·1 in 1947, 27·4 in 1948. In Malaya the annual
rate of natural growth was about 24 per thousand in 1947–8.
It is more than 20 per thousand in the Philippines, in Thai-
land, Taiwan, Korea, China, and about 25 and 26 per
thousand in Southern and Central America.

From a demographic point of view, all that 'exploding'
underdeveloped countries need is to bring down their birth-
rates to a manageable level. But the reduction of birth-rates
is in some way related to substantial improvement in the
levels of living. And these improvements are the more difficult to obtain the greater the population pressure is. If
capital output ratio is 3, i.e. 3 units of capital are required to
produce one unit of income, then with a population growth
of 2 per cent per annum, 6 per cent of the net income has
yearly to be invested only to maintain the same level of
living for the increased population. With a population
growth of 3 per cent per annum, 9 per cent of national
income has to be invested to reach the same result.[1] The
higher the rate of population growth, the harder becomes
the task of breaking through a Malthusian trap.[2] A vicious
spiral is therefore set into operation. Because of a high rate
of population growth, 'industrialization' is difficult to attain.
Because there is no 'industrialization' the birth-rate and the
rate of population growth remain high. A solution must
certainly come. As has been said, there is a long-run incompatibility between high fertility rates and low death-
rates. No matter what technological progress the future
brings, in the long run either fertility rates must be reduced

1. Brand, 1959, p. 28.
2. Tinbergen, 1956, p. 91 : 'a reduction in population growth will
also be of considerable help in stepping up production *per capita*
for the simple reason that there will be more available per head if
there are less heads.'

or mortality rates must increase.[1] An equilibrium must be reached. But when will it be reached. And how?

1. Coale, 1959, p. 36.

CHAPTER 5

How Many People?

POPULATION GROWTH AND STANDARDS OF LIVING

'MY first approach to the population problem was purely mathematical. But it immediately became apparent that in its real essence the problem was a biological one. This conclusion led to its controlled experimental study in the laboratory.' With these words a well-known American scientist, Pearl, began an epoch-making book on *The Biology of Population Growth*, published a few decades ago.

The study he referred to was conducted in a laboratory with a 'suitable creature', *Drosophila melanoguster*. 'It is a small fly, which looks like a diminutive replica of a common house fly, and is seen in swarms around decaying or fermenting fruit, or liquids like cider and vinegar made from fruit and left exposed to the air.' He selected a group – 'Adam and Eve, a few young children (larvae) and a few older children (pupae)' – and enclosed them in a special bottle with appropriate food. Thus he arranged 'a dipteran microcosm, a spatially limited but well-equipped universe'. And he set himself to watch 'nature take her accustomed course'.

'In due time more children will be born, since mère and père are no slackers in the chiefest of biological duties and privileges. Some will die. Others will grow up and have offspring of their own. Ultimately the old folks will pass away, but not before there has accumulated around them a great crowd of their descendants of several generations. In short a population will have grown in this little universe.' From censuses of the 'population' at frequent intervals, about every second or third day, the experimenter concluded that 'the fly *Drosophila* in its population growth under controlled experimental conditions follows the logistic curve' (see Fig. 8).

Pearl then spent endless efforts to demonstrate that the growth of human population likewise adheres to the patterns of the logistic curve. And since there are always many

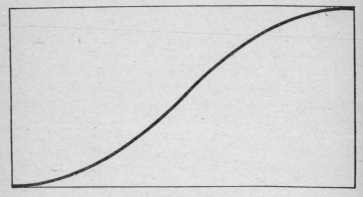

Fig. 8. The logistic curve

people very fond of using simple mathematical tools to explain complex social phenomena, the thesis of the eminent geneticist became quite popular.

Actually, any generalization from Pearl's experiment is rather questionable.[1] The growth of a human population has peculiar elements that differentiate it from the growth of, say, a population of *Drosophila melanogaster*. It is sufficient

1. For a critical appraisal of Pearl's experiments, see Coontz, 1957, pp. 36–42.

to remember the unequal distribution of incomes and resources among the human population and the fact that man has learned how to control and to increase, at least within certain limits, the supply of food and resources at his disposal, thereby enlarging through technological and organizational progress the 'bottle' in which he happens to live.

It cannot be denied that Pearl's experiments vividly demonstrate how a given population of living creatures may tend to expand to the limit of available resources. However, it has recently been demonstrated that in the social life of many species of superior animals some sort of 'territorial rights' are enforced that prevent the entire species from facing a Malthusian situation. In these cases the burden of Malthusian pressure is made to fall upon a minority of displaced and destitute individuals, and the population is maintained noticeably below the maximum possible density.[1] It can easily be proved that 'territoriality' operates also among men.[2] Furthermore, in the behaviour of human population there are other elements of distinct originality. *Drosophila melanogaster* uses the supply of agar in the bottle just to increase its number. Man uses available re-

1. 'Territoriality' has been discovered by observing the social behaviour of birds and mammals. The effects of 'territoriality' on population have been summarized as follows: 'Should the population increase, local population density does not continue to build up indefinitely. Instead territorial defence forces individuals out into marginal situations, and thus the resources of the optimal habitat are not exhausted. Most of the displaced individuals do not survive, but some may find unexploited areas of suitable habitat and thus extend the range of the species. The result is that population tends to be maintained at or below the optimum density in the preferred habitat, and the excess individuals are forced to marginal areas to which they must adapt or die.' (Bartholomew and Birdsell, 1953, p. 485.)

2. Forde,1953, pp. 373–4; Bates, 1955, 68–76.

sources to increase his numbers, *and* to improve his levels of living. The 'ceiling' to population growth in human societies – at least in non-savage ones – is set 'not by the carrying capacity at a subsistence level, but by the carrying capacity at a desired or conventional standard of living.'[1]

Which are the mechanisms that allocate resources between the two alternative uses – population growth and better levels of living? The question is still open to discussion. Unequal distribution of income undoubtedly played a key role in ancient societies. The emergence of privileged classes of priests and aristocrats has since the earliest days of human history diverted resources to higher modes of living and prevented the increase of available production from being fully absorbed by the growth of population. Uneven distribution of income and the very fact that the rate of growth of industrial production remained noticeably above the rate of population growth for a long period must have been key factors during the Industrial Revolution in establishing the higher standards of living that compete with the natural propensity to have children. Imitation of upper classes by lower classes or of 'developed' by 'underdeveloped' societies should also be taken into proper account in this regard.

Whatever the causes and the mechanisms, it is abundantly clear that, since its appearance on this planet, human society has increased its size *and* bettered its levels of living. There is of course the question whether the allocation of available resources between 'quantity' and 'quality' has been the best one. We shall discuss this problem later on. Let us for the moment try to assess the quantitative growth.

1. Taylor, 1956, p. 50.

THE AGRICULTURAL REVOLUTION

It was pointed out in Chapter 1 that all available evidence seems to show that around 10,000 B.C. all – or almost all – the human population on this planet still lived by hunting, fishing, and gathering wild fruits. Chapter 4 then explained that a society of hunters or fishers rarely reaches an average density of 2·5 persons per square mile. Working on those suppositions, and taking into account the fact that some areas of the Earth are not inhabitable, one can reasonably suppose that on the eve of the Agricultural Revolution there could not have been more than 20 million people on earth. This figure has to be regarded as the maximum. The minimum can be credibly fixed around 2 million. The actual population probably ranged between 5 and 10 million people.[1]

The Agricultural Revolution allowed the species to break this ceiling. Man enlarged Pearl's bottle, and human population increased far beyond any previously possible level. Although the demographic increase can properly be visualized as a consequence of the Agricultural Revolution, one should not overlook the fact that the growth of population may have in its turn fostered the diffusion of the Revolution. Neolithic people migrated in search of cultivable lands and in so doing broadcast the basic Neolithic discovery. Migrations occurred because of the turn-over, plant, move-on type of primitive agriculture. They may also have occurred because of demographic pressure.

A very illuminating example is represented by the arrival of the first 'farmers' on the coasts of England. We are in-

1. Huxley, 1957, p. 172; Durand, 1958, p. 29; Deevey, 1960, pp. 196–7.

debted to Professor Piggott for a masterly account of these ancient developments.

The primitive farmers arrived in isolated and generally small bands at various points on the southern coast of England at various times between 2000 and 1500 B.C. They came from various regions of the Atlantic and Channel coasts of Western Europe. 'They must have brought with them not only the knowledge and skills of the agriculturalist, but the actual seed corn and domesticated beasts of their flocks and herds, as well as some portable belongings – bow and arrows, spears, axes, hoes, tinder and fire-making materials – from their homeland. . . . It is likely that little or no opposition would be received from the scattered and migratory population – the land was large enough for all, and there was no competition in the two divergent ways of life of the farmer and the hunter. . . . The first Neolithic colonists of Britain encountered then a Mesolithic population likely to have been very small numerically, probably largely moving in seasonal migrations, having semi-permanent camps and settlements. . . . It is difficult to detect signs of contact between the two groups – aboriginal hunter-fishers and immigrant agriculturalists – in the British Isles during what must have been the first phases of colonization in the various regions. At Glecknabae in Bute a Clyde-Carlingford chambered tomb overlay a midden of shells, undated but likely to have been a product of local Mesolithic folk, and over this a turf-line had formed before the building of the cairn; at Thickthorn in Dorset a long barrow overlay a pit probably of Mesolithic origin; and here again sealed by a turf-line. Neither instance really demonstrates any relationship between the two groups of cultures.

'The material culture of the immigrant agriculturalists which can on various grounds be assigned to an early phase of settlement seems invariably to represent the introduction of completely novel equipment, and there are no signs that an immediate fusion took place with the Mesolithic traditions. But in various regional cultures in Britain which can be shown to belong to a later phase, elements derived from indigenous Mesolithic sources can be detected, often contributing very strikingly to the make-up and producing distinctive insular variants of Neolithic culture unknown on the Continent. Such a state of affairs is only to be expected – the introduction of a completely novel mode of living based on agriculture and stock-breeding, with its accompanying material equipment, from the European mainland, and the subsequent absorption into this of the residual elements of the old hunter-fisher traditions which it largely, but not wholly, supplanted.' [1]

The demographic growth that accompanied and followed the Agricultural Revolution usually expressed itself – at least in the first stages – in a multiplication of settlements rather than in the enlargement of the settlement unit. In prehistoric Europe the largest Neolithic village yet known – Barkaer, in Jutland – cannot have included more than 300 or 400 people. The middle Neolithic village on the shores of the Federsee in South Württemberg, Germany, had no more than twenty-five houses, twenty to thirty feet long by about fifteen feet wide.

Later on, in the course of time, with the emergence of higher modes of life, improved productive techniques and organizations, and higher civilizations, population densities increased very noticeably, and towns and large villages appeared – much more extensive than the ancient camps of the early Neolithic peoples. Yet one has to keep in mind

1. Piggott, 1954, pp. 15–16.

that, until the Industrial Revolution, everywhere in the world, towns with more than 100 thousand people remained extremely rare. Big figures are often quoted, but they generally represent gross exaggerations. As late as the sixteenth century, in Europe an average town numbered from 5 to 20 thousand people and any agglomeration with more than 20 thousand inhabitants was considered a big town.[1] Throughout the ages, in any part of the world, the story of agricultural societies remained essentially the story of numerous small, more or less isolated microcosms.

It has been indicated that, on the eve of the Agricultural Revolution, around 10,000 B.C., the human species must have amounted to anything between 2 and 20 million people.

On the eve of the Industrial Revolution, around A.D. 1750, the total world population must have ranged between 650 and 850 million people. And it is probably correct to say that about 80 per cent of that population was concentrated in Eurasia (see Table 16).

There are a number of reasons that lead us to believe that the total reached in 1750 had never been approached before. The 750 ± 100 million figure is in a way the 'historical' maximum for the agricultural phase of the story of man. The 'theoretical' maximum could have been much higher with better distribution of income, more efficient productive organization, and diffusion of advanced agricultural practices and new kinds of crops into various agricultural areas and into the strongholds of the last Paleolithic hunters (especially in the Americas and Australia). In fact, there are clear indications that the human species was still expanding.

1. Mols. 1955, Part 2, p. 41.

Between 1650 and 1750, world population was probably growing at a rate of 0.3–0.4 per cent per year.[1]

TABLE 16. *Estimates of world population, 1750–1950*
(numbers in millions)

	Area (Km²)	1750	1850	1950
World total	135	750 ± 100	1200 ± 100	2476 (± 5%)
Africa	30	100 (?)	100 (?)	199
America	42	15 ± 5	60 ± 10	330
Asia	27	500 ± 50	750 ± 50	1360
Europe	5	120 ± 10	210	393
Oceania	9	2 (?)	2	13
U.S.S.R.	22	30 ± 5	60 ± 5	190

These estimates for 1750 and 1850 represent a revised version of the estimates by Willcox and Carr Saunders. The totals for 1950 are adjusted estimates of the mid-year population as calculated in U.N. *Demographic Yearbook*, 1956, p. 151.

THE INDUSTRIAL REVOLUTION

Then came the Industrial Revolution. And population exploded. Once again, much of the material gain obtained by man in mastering his environment was absorbed by increase in numbers.

The previous chapter illustrated the mechanism of the demographic explosion brought about by the Industrial Revolution. Now, let us assess the result of this explosion. In 1750 the total world population ranged somewhere between 650 and 850 million people. In 1850 it was between 1100 and 1300 million. In 1900 it was around 1600 million. In 1950 it was in the neighbourhood of 2500 million (see Table 16), and it is now increasing much faster than ever. The

1. U.N., 1953, p. 12. For the remarkable growth of Chinese population from 1680 to 1775 see Ping-Ti Ho, 1959, pp. 266–70.

average annual rate of growth was about 0·7 per cent in 1850–1900 and about 1 per cent in 1900–50. Today it is about 1·7 per cent. Every year there is now a net addition

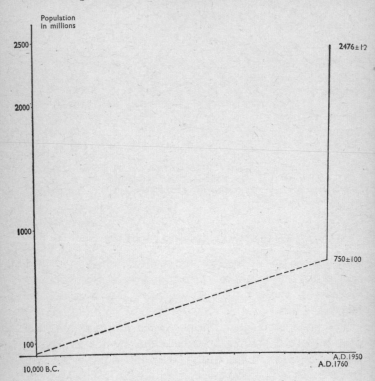

Fig. 9. The growth of world human population, 10,000 B.C. to A.D. 1950

of more than 40 million individuals. A biologist, looking at the diagram showing the recent growth of world population in a long-range perspective (see Fig. 9), said that he had the impression of being in the presence of the growth-curve of a microbe population in a body suddenly struck by some infectious disease. The 'bacillus' man is taking over the world.[1]

EXODUS FROM EUROPE

The demographic explosion did not take place simultaneously all over the globe. It started in Europe – because the Industrial Revolution started there.

Around 1750 the population of Europe (including European Russia) must have been around 145 million people. It was about 265 million in 1850, about 400 million in 1900, and about 550 million in 1950.[2] These figures, however, do not tell the entire story. Under the push of internal demographic pressure and with the advantage of technological superiority – which in one form appeared in superior military power – the Europeans spread all over the world, peacefully and otherwise. They settled in the Americas and Australia. And they came to control Africa and Asia. 'The great exodus from Europe has been the most important migratory movement of the modern era, and perhaps the largest in all human history.[3]

Today, that expansion still arouses violent emotions

1. At a growth rate of 1·7 per cent per annum, the world population, estimated at 2700 million in 1956, will double in 40 years. If the same rate continues, by 2156 world population will be 86·4 milliard and in 700 years from 1956 there will be one person per square meter on the earth (sea area included). It seems evident that such a rate of population increase as now prevails cannot continue. Even if one is relatively optimistic about actual and potential natural resources of the world and the effect of developments of technology on the production of food and other necessities, it is abundantly clear that in the not distant future either the world birth-rate has to go down, or the death-rate has to go up. See Brand, 1959, p. 27.

2. U.N., 1953, p. 11.   3. U.N., 1953, p. 98.

around the world. Many peoples fought it fiercely and there is no doubt that European expansion often assumed crude tones of exploitation and oppression. But it is not difficult to maintain that it was less cruel and bloody than most other 'expansions' in human history. There was something epic in a migration that saw Europeans spreading all over the world – building railroads, creating towns and harbours, opening canals, settling desert areas, bringing new lands under cultivation, and building factories, hospitals, missions, and universities.

Average annual overseas emigration from Europe amounted to *circa* 377 thousand individuals per year in the period 1846–90, somewhat around 911 thousand in 1891–1920, and about 366 thousand in 1921–9.[1] On the whole, between 1846 and 1930 over 50 million Europeans sought new homes overseas.[2] The bulk of this emigration was to North America, chiefly to the United States. Of some 20 million persons born in Europe and living in other Continents in 1930, nearly 14 million were in North America, about 5 million in Latin America (chiefly Argentina and Brazil), and something more than 1 million in Australia and South Africa.[3]

The growing relative importance of the 'European stock' until the first half of the twentieth century can best be illustrated by the following figures. According to calculations by Professor Kuczynski,[4] the 'white or Caucasian' population of the Earth was nearly 200 million in 1800, and about 700 million in 1930. Total world population was respectively about 910 and 2010 million.[5] This means that the Caucasian

1. U.N., 1953, p. 100.
2. Carr-Saunders, 1936, p. 49, and Kirk, 1946, pp. 72–96.
3. U.N., 1953, p. 101.   4. Kuczynski, 1934, Vol. 12, pp. 240–8.
5. U.N., 1953, p. 11.

Table 17. World population in 1955

	Population mid-year 1955 (millions)	Birth (rates ‰)	Death (rates ‰)	Population growth (rates)	Population growth (millions)	Percentage distribution of enumerated population by age under 15	15–59	60 and over
WORLD	2691	34	18	16	42·6	34	58	8
AFRICA								
North Africa	78	45	25	20	1·5	39	55	6
Tropical and South	145	45	25	20	2·8	43	49	6
AMERICA								
North America	183	25	9	17	3·0	27	61	12
Middle America	58	45	19	26	1·4	42	53	6
South America	125	40	17	25	3·0	39	56	5
ASIA								
South West	73	42	22	20	1·4	38	56	6
South Central	499	41	28	13	6·3	37	57	6
South East	185	45	28	17	3·0	43	53	4
East	724	35	16	19	13·3	37	56	7
EUROPE								
North and West	137	18	11	6	0·8	24	61	15
Central	134	20	11	9	1·2	24	62	14
Southern	138	21	10	10	1·4	28	61	9
OCEANIA	15	25	8	22	0·3	30	61	12
U.S.S.R.	197	26	9	17	3·2			

Source: *Demographic Yearbook 1956*, pp. 2 and 8. (The results of the Soviet census for 1959 seem to indicate that the estimate of 197 million for the U.S.S.R. in 1955 is probably exaggerated.)

population was about 22 per cent of the human species in 1800, and about 35 per cent in 1930.

FEEDING NEW MOUTHS

The diffusion of white people all over the world fostered the diffusion of the Industrial Revolution – just as the migration of early Neolithic farmers had fostered the diffusion of the Agricultural Revolution. The opening of the North-American West, the first cotton mills of Bombay, the first railroads of Argentina or of China, were all phenomena strictly connected with European expansion.

Today the first round of world demographic explosion is over. Europe, North America, and Russia have reached or are reaching the demographic equilibrium of 'industrial' type – with low death- and low birth-rates. We are now facing the second round, which promises to be even more explosive than the first. Asia, South America, and Africa are undergoing a demographic growth of unprecedented magnitude. Their rates of growth range between 1·5 per cent and 2·5 per cent per year (see Table 17).

The previous chapter illustrates the mechanism of the demographic explosion of the 'underdeveloped' areas. Here we may consider its economic implications. An example in point is India. It is estimated that around 1918 India had about 315 million people. The average annual quantity of food grain available to the Indian population was then about 20 ounces *per capita*. By 1945 India's population had increased to about 400 million people. The average daily quantity of food-grains available *per capita* had correspondingly fallen to about 15 ounces. After 1945 the situation further worsened and *per capita* food supply diminished substantially between 1945 and 1952.[1] Today, big projects are carried on for long-range agricultural development. All the related massive investments will possibly stop the further worsening of the situation. But because of the high rate of growth of the consuming population there is no likelihood that, despite all efforts, agricultural output *per capita* can increase spectacularly.[2] It is a typical case of a Malthusian trap. Unfortunately it is not the only one. 'One who has seen poverty and its concomitants in rural areas in India, China, or Egypt does not doubt the reality of Malthusian checks, even though he may cavil at Malthusian arithmetic.'[3]

In this regard one has to remember that countries now in the industrial stage experienced the demographic explosion together with and because of the Industrial Revolution. Demographic growth in those cases has been just one aspect of a more complex and balanced aggregate of changes. If the Industrial Revolution brought around more mouths to be fed, it also somehow gave the means to feed them.[4]

But in many 'underdeveloped' societies today the situation is completely different. The fall in the death-rate does not occur as part of a balanced aggregate of changes, but as the product of changes that matured elsewhere. For these countries there is only one solution – to undergo the Industrial Revolution.

Future economic historians may say that demographic growth represented a challenge to the 'underdeveloped'

1. Bhattacharjee, 1958, p. 198; Coale and Hoover, 1958, p. 86 ff.; *Ford Foundation*, 1959. While considering the figures quoted in the text one should keep in mind that food grains account for at least 75 per cent of the calorie intake in India.

2. Coale and Hoover, 1958, p. 110.   3. Belshaw, 1956, p. 10 n.

4. When it gave them no possibility of being fed at home it gave them the possibility to 'expand' – more or less peacefully – all over the globe.

world to quicken the pace of industrialization. But looking at things here and now, one is frightened by the magnitude and difficulty of the problem that demographic pressure is creating. Backward societies are faced with problems much more critical than those that faced old Europe. They *must* do things quickly. They *must* do things on a greater scale. The scale of their demographic growth impels them to quicker and greater capital accumulation. They have no 'empty' or 'underdeveloped' spaces to go to.

A solution will certainly come. But which? And where will the overall growth of human population eventually stop?

CHAPTER 6

An Age of Transition

IT is a leitmotiv in this book that the three basic types of economic organization – hunting, agricultural, industrial – are accompanied by three corresponding ranges of economic and demographic levels at which human societies operate. The previous chapters were devoted to the assessment of these ranges. Now we have to deal with the notion that the passage of a society from one type of economic organization to another also implies some drastic cultural and social changes.

We are in a good position to detect the relevance of such changes, for we ourselves live in an age of transition. Three generations ago more than two thirds of the people living on the earth were peasants. In three generations, less than one third will live 'in the fields'. The Industrial Revolution is spreading all over the world. We witness that the changes are 'not merely industrial but also social and intellectual'.[1] We witness that the technological revolution is accompanied – as Stendhal noticed – by a revolution *'dans les habitudes, les idées, les croyances'*.[2] A new style of life is emerging, as another disappears for ever.

Every aspect of life has to be geared to the new modes of production. Family ties are on the wane and give way to broader perspectives for larger social groups. Individual saving gives way to collective social services, undistributed profits, and taxes. The all-rounded philosophical education of the few is set aside in favour of the technical training of

1. Ashton, 1950, p. 2.
2. Stendhal, 1925, Vol. 1, p. 91.

the many. Artistic intuition must give way to technical precision. New juridical institutions, new types of ownership and management, different distributions of income, new tastes, new values, new ideals have to emerge as an essential part of the industrialization process.

Actually, when 'industrialization' occurs gradually, these socio-cultural changes take place in a balanced process with economic changes. But when, as in many backward areas today, 'industrialization' is artificially speeded up, the socio-cultural environment may show a much greater degree of resistance to change than the economic structure. If such is the case, the static socio-cultural environment can indeed represent a formidable bottleneck and invalidate all efforts to achieve industrialization. This is the reason why some of those societies who want, or are forced, to quicken the pace of industrialization may feel – more or less emotionally – the urge to resort to political and social revolutionary movements. The socio-political revolution is a rough way to break through the socio-cultural bottleneck. All the miseries and the hardships that follow then become part of the price of industrialization.

EDUCATION IN A TECHNICAL AGE

In Chapter 3 I mentioned some of these pointers that show the levels to which an industrial society may attain. There is no doubt that industrialization brings with it an extraordinary improvement in the average material standard of living. It is not to be supposed from all this that the industrial world must necessarily be a good one. There is nothing in the mechanism of the spread of the Industrial Revolution which guarantees *a priori* that the material result will be used for good ends. Unless mankind makes an enormous effort of self-education the possibility that the Industrial Revolution may eventually come to represent a disastrous calamity for the human race cannot be altogether excluded.

'We have not yet been installed for long in this landscape of mines and power stations; we have not long begun to live in this new home which we have not yet finished building. Everything has changed so quickly around us: human relationships, working conditions, customs. Our very psychology has been shaken to its most intimate recesses. . . .

'We are all of us young barbarians still amazed at our own inventions. To the colonialist the meaning of life is given by conquest. The soldier despises the farmer, but is not the installing of this same farmer the aim itself of conquest? In the excitement of our progress we have used men to build railways, raise factories, and bore wells for oil, and have forgotten that we did all this to serve men themselves. During the time of the conquest our morale was a soldier's morale, but now we have to colonize we have to make this new home, that has not yet acquired a countenance, alive and human. For one generation the problem was to build; for the other the problem is how to live there.'[1]

Huxley, Fromm, White,[2] and others have repeatedly warned us about the dangers of conformism and mental sickness that weigh upon an industrialized society. The mass schools of the 'industrial' world tend to teach 'techniques' that leave the spirit barren. The intellectuals that proliferate from the 'industrial' mass universities more and more come to resemble the drab figures of the mass scientists depicted by Ortega y Gasset.[3] With technological progress, it becomes

1. A. de Saint Exupéry, 1939, pp. 65–7.
2. Fromm, 1956; White, 1956; A. Huxley, 1958.
3. Ortega y Gasset, 1932, Chapter 12, pp. 119–26.

day by day more and more easy for unscrupulous or irresponsible individuals to control powerful forces that allow them to influence or even direct the behaviour of the people.

How much of all this is inescapably tied to industrialization? How much of this can be avoided by a greater effort in education? Analysis of private expenditure in the United States, the United Kingdom, France, Germany, Italy, Denmark, Belgium, and the Netherlands shows that in each of these countries people spend more on tobacco and drink than on education. Actually, adjustment should be made to arrive at meaningful comparisons. Account should be taken of the need to feed and clothe those receiving education during the period in which they make no direct contribution to output. To assess the proportion of real resources diverted to education through private expenditure one should also make allowance for the effect of indirect taxation. All considered, however, there is no doubt that the current structure of private expenditure discloses disturbing scales of values. It also indicates a high propensity on the part of the family to throw on the society the responsibility for the education of the new generations.

The family nucleus is losing its strength in the industrial world, but it will not disappear altogether. Parents must be aware and constantly reminded of their immense cultural responsibilities. A good education presupposes enormous investment. No collective services, benefits, or schools can substitute for the family in this endeavour.

'Even if all the members of the educated minority had succeeded in rising above their natural human egotism and had tried with all their might to share their cultural heritage with the unprivileged majority of their fellow human beings, they would have been defeated before the Industrial Revolution by the smallness of the economic surplus remaining in hand after the satisfaction of elementary economic needs. . . . In the pre-industrial agricultural economy in which human and animal muscle power has not been reinforced by mechanical power, all but a small minority of the members of society are condemned to live as a peasantry whose puny production cannot provide amenities beyond such common necessities as food, clothing, and shelter for more than a small minority. . . . An injustice that has long since been intolerable has now been made unnecessary by the Industrial Revolution which has brought it within our economic power"[1] at last to provide education for mankind in the mass.

This we are doing, at least in industrial societies. We also have to be careful, however, about *how* we are doing it. The uneducated or semi-educated masses can increasingly influence culture and a wave of vulgarity can pervade philosophy and art. I am fully convinced that this is a price that we are inescapably bound to pay. But I am also convinced that much can be done to reduce this price. Large social investments can be devoted to the education of the many so that their damaging influence on culture will be noticeably reduced. Heavy investment on the part of individual families on a broad and gentle education for their children should also make the survival of cultural élites possible. This combined effort of family and society may indeed mitigate the drab destiny foreseen by Huxley: a vulgar civilization of semi-educated people, enslaved by inhuman forms of anonymous tyranny and agglomerated 'in cities of interminable monotonies, of hopeless dreariness, and suffocating oppression'.

1. Toynbee, 1960, p. 62.

MAN'S BIOLOGICAL PAST

There is another, perhaps more fundamental problem, which again only good and diffused education can help to solve. For more than nine-tenths of its existence, the entire human race has lived in a state of complete savagery. Only very recently, with the discovery of agriculture, has man started on a different course. The events that followed the first Revolution were cumulative. After the supply of biological sources of energy – animals and plants – had been brought under control, other sources were mastered, while the accumulation of knowledge allowed a progressively more efficient exploitation of the newly-conquered energy. The greater the control man acquired over his environment, the greater became his opportunity to extend it.

Ten thousand years may seem a very long span of time, but, from the point of view of the whole history of the earth and mankind, ten thousand years is a very brief fragment. It is truly extraordinary that in about ten thousand years *homo sapiens* has turned himself from a savage into the conqueror not only of this world but also of outer space. This accomplishment actually looks even more remarkable if instead of measuring the time involved by our usual chronological standard – the solar year – we measure it in terms of generations. Considering that the Neolithic Revolution diffused into Europe between 5000 B.C. and 2000 B.C., and assuming for a generation a period of about twenty-five years, slightly more than 150 generations separate each European from his 'nasty and brutish' ancestor.

Here, in fact, lies the great question. Because of a cumulative process, the technical progress of *homo sapiens* has been extremely rapid. In a relatively small number of generations, man has come to control his environment and to master the most powerful forces of Nature. But how much has he himself improved in quality?

There is no escaping man's origin – a carnivorous and cannibalistic animal – and disgustingly so. Dr Marais, Dr P. J. van B. Viljoen, and Dr Uys Pienaar, 'are emphatic that no other carnivore will devour a hyena's carcass. They assure us that, on the contrary, they have frequently encountered the mummified carcasses of hyenas in the veld; the carcasses often lie untouched by bird or beast where they have been shot or cast aside from traps. This revulsion against eating hyena flesh was not experienced by human beings such as the ancient Europeans. However nauseating hyena flesh may be to hyenas and to other carnivorous creatures, man, the greatest of all scavengers, whether presapient or sapient, could cope with the flesh of any and every competitor – even if it happened to be his own flesh and blood. Hyena bones are associated with most anthropological discoveries. They were found with rhinoceros and human bones and fragments of pottery in an early discovery made in the cavern at Pondres, near Nîmes, Gard (France), by De Christol in 1829; almost a century later, accompanying human implements of Mousterian (or lower Aurignacian) type in Shensi, China; accompanying the remains of *Sinanthropus* at Choukoutien; and with *Australopithecus prometheus* at Makapansgat.[1]

A modern optimistic writer, while admitting that 'cannibalism has been a common practice until recently' is emphatic that 'eating your dead enemy or drinking his blood from his empty skull has been a mark of greatest admiration and wish to acquire his virtue. It was a spiritual acknowledgement from the first and in symbolic form survives even in Christian communion.'[2] I fear that there are

1. Dart, 1959, pp. 127–8. 2. Berrill, 1957, p. 85.

and always have been very few creatures who would welcome this kind of 'spiritual acknowledgement'. But apart from this, it seems to me that we have to be careful not to confuse the logic of the events. It is not that the crimes of man are bound to have a mark of 'spirituality', but rather that even when man tried to do something 'spiritual', he was bound to show the mark of his origin.

For thousands and thousands of years, for more than nine tenths of man's existence, the most cruel selective process progressively worsened the situation, only partially counteracted by the 'good' factor of 'cooperation'. So man evolved – the 'creature fashioned around and selected for hunting . . . the creature whose biological capacities are geared to the life of a hunter'.[1]

The selective process that favoured the success and the multiplication of the aggressive type was certainly not interrupted by the Neolithic Revolution. It continued to operate well into 'civilized' times and to a large extent still operates today, when man can command immensely powerful forces, and his efficiency – for good or for evil – has increased in spectacular fashion. A single man or a small group of individuals – as recent history has dramatically demonstrated – can today bring about unspeakable catastrophes that affect not this or that group, this or that region, but the entire world and the entire human species.

It is disturbing to see that still today, even in the most advanced countries, in large sections of human society, aggressiveness is praised as a virtue – or at least as a valuable asset. We need a crusade against violence and aggressiveness. We need – more than anything else – to educate people to tolerance and gentility. As H. G. Wells once said, the future of mankind depends on the outcome of a race

1. Coon, 1958, pp. 8 and 212.

between education and catastrophe. We need to improve the quality of man.

QUALITY OR QUANTITY?

Improvement in quality of the human species is not necessarily alternative to a growth in quantity. A larger population may mean greater possibilities in the division of labour and economies of scale. These possibilities may contribute to the growth of *per capita* income, to better levels of living, and to better education. But beyond certain points, quantity and quality may well become competitive. The question whether the allocation of available resources between quantity and quality has been on the whole well done in the history of mankind, is impossible to answer. Among other things it implies the objectively impossible assessment of all kinds of ethical and cultural values and standards. Some facts, though, may perhaps help to give at least a general idea about what the general tendency has been. When the Neolithic Revolution occurred about ten thousand years ago, there were – as we have seen – far less than 20 million people on the earth. Today, there are more than 2700 million. Now, of the adult portion of this population, about 50 per cent are absolutely illiterate (see Table 18). A mere glance at these figures immediately suggests that far too much of the available resources was used up by the quantitative increase of mankind at the expense of its qualitative improvement.

We must invest more of our resources to the qualitative improvement of man. As Julian Huxley once said, we must place meaningful quality above meaningless quantity. There must be a combined effort in both the public and the private sectors toward such a goal. In this regard it should be

TABLE 18. *Estimated adult literacy rates in the world population,*
1950

	Estimated population 15 years old and over (millions)	Estimated adult literacy rates (per cent)
WORLD	1587	55–57
AFRICA		
North Africa	40	10–15
Tropical and South	80	15–20
AMERICA		
North America	126	96–97
Middle America	30	58–60
South America	67	56–58
ASIA		
South West	37	20–25
South Central	287	15–20
South East	102	30–35
East	404	50–55
EUROPE		
North & West	102	98–99
Central	96	97–98
South	95	79–80
U.S.S.R.	112	89–90
OCEANIA	9	90–95

Source: UNESCO, 1957, p. 15.

remembered that what is needed is not merely more technical knowledge. What man today desperately needs is the
kind of education that allows him to make a wise use of the
techniques he possesses. 'We live at a time when man, Lord
of all things, is not Lord of himself. He feels lost amid his
own abundance. . . . To modern man is happening what was
said of the Regent during the minority of Louis XV: he
had all the talents except the talent to make use of
them.'[1]

1. Ortega y Gasset, 1932, p. 47.

For underdeveloped countries intensive and well organized educational schemes must be quickly developed. Educational assistance has to accompany or even precede technical and economic aid. There is nothing more dangerous than technical knowledge when unaccompanied by respect for human life and human values. The introduction of modern techniques in environments that are still dominated by intolerance and aggressiveness is a most alarming development. Urgent action is needed lest the last state turn out to be worse than the first.

Bibliography

ALEATI, G., 1957. *La popolazione di Pavia durante il dominio spagnuolo*. Milano.

ALSBERG, C., 1948. *Chemistry and the Theory of Population*. Stanford, California.

AMAR, J., 1920. *The Human Motor*. London.

ASHTON, T. S., 1950. *The Industrial Revolution*. London.

AUKRUST, O., 1959. 'Investment and Economic Growth', *Productivity Measurement Review*, 16.

AYRES, E., and SCARLOTT, C. A., 1952. *Energy Sources*. New York, Toronto, London.

BAILLOUD, G., 1955. *Les Civilisations néolithiques de la France dans leur contexte européen*. Paris.

BARK, W. C., 1958. *Origins of the Medieval World*. Stanford, California.

BARNETT, R. D., 1958. 'Early Shipping in the Near East', *Antiquity*, 32.

BARTHOLOMEW, G. A., and BIRDSELL, J. B., 1953, 'Ecology and the Protohominids', *American Anthropologist*, 55.

BATES, M., 1953. 'Human ecology', *Anthropology Today* (ed. A. L. Kroeber). Chicago.

1955. *The Prevalence of People*. New York.

BAUER, P. T., and YAMEY, B. S., 1951. 'Economic Progress and Occupational Distribution', *Economic Journal*, 61.

BAUM, V. A., 1955. 'Prospects for the Application of Solar Energy and some Research Results in the U.S.S.R.', *Proceedings of the World Symposium on Applied Solar Energy*. Phoenix, Arizona.

BELLIDO, A. G., 1955. 'La vida media en la España romana', *Revista intern. do sociologia*, 13.

BELSHAW, H., 1956. *Population Growth and Levels of Consumption*.

BENNETT, M. K., 1951. 'International Disparities in Consumption Levels', *American Economic Review*, 41.

BERRILL, N. J., 1957. *Man's Emerging Mind*. New York.

BHATTACHARJEE, J. P., and associates, 1958. 'Trend of Consumption of Food and Foodgrains in India', *Tenth International*

118

BIBLIOGRAPHY

Conference of Agricultural Economists, ed. J. P. Bhattacharjee. Bombay.

BIRD, J. R., 1948. 'Pre-ceramic Cultures in Chicama and Viru', *American Antiquity*, 13, 4, Part II.

BISHOP, C. W., 1933. 'The Neolithic Age in Northern China', *Antiquity*, 7.

BLOCH, M., 1935. 'Avènement et conquêtes du moulin à eau', *Annales d'histoire économique et sociale*, 7.

1935. 'Les Inventions médiévales', *Annales d'histoire économique et sociale*, 7.

BORAZ, J., 1959. 'First Tools in Mankind', *Natural History*.

BRAIDWOOD, R. J., 1957. *Prehistoric Man*. Chicago.

1960. 'The Agricultural Revolution', *Scientific American*.

BRAIDWOOD, R. J., and REED, C. A., 1957. 'The Achievement and Early Consequences of Food Production', Cold Spring Harbor Symposia on Quantitative Biology. Vol. 22. *Population Studies: Animal Ecology and Demography*. New York.

BRAND, W., 1959. 'The World Population Problem', *International Population Conference*. Vienna.

BROWN, H., 1954. *The Challenge of Man's Future*. New York.

BURDFORD, A., 1960. 'Heavy Transport in Classical Antiquity', *Economic History Review*, 13.

BURKITT, M., 1956. *The Old Stone Age*. New York.

BURN, A. R., 1953. 'Hic breve vivitur. A Study of the Expectation of Life in the Roman Empire', *Past and Present*, 4.

CARR-SAUNDERS, A. M., 1936. *World Population*. Oxford.

CARUS-WILSON, E. M., 1941. 'An Industrial Revolution of the Thirteenth Century', *Economic History Review*, 11.

C.E.C.A., 1957. *Studio sulla struttura e tendenze dell'economia energetica nel paesi della Comunità*. Luxembourg.

CHASTELAND, J. C., 1960. 'Évolution générale de la mortalité en Europe Occidentale de 1900 à 1950', *Population*, 15.

CLARK, C., 1957. *The Conditions of Economic Progress*. London.

COALE, A. J., 1959. 'Increases in Expectation of Life and Population Growth', *International Population Conference*. Vienna.

COALE, A. J., and HOOVER, E. M., 1958. *Population Growth and Economic Development in Low-Income Countries*. Princeton.

COLE, S., 1954. *The Prehistory of East Africa*. Hardmondsworth.

BIBLIOGRAPHY

COON, C. S., 1957. *The Seven Caves*. New York.
1958. *The Story of Man*. New York.

COONTZ, S. H., 1957. *Population Theories and their Economic Interpretation*. London.

COTTRELL, F., 1955. *Energy and Society*. New York, Toronto, London.

DART, R. A., 1959. *Adventures with the Missing Link*. New York.

DARWIN, C. G., 1953. *The Next Million Years*. New York.

DAVIS, K., 1951. 'Population and the Further Spread of Industrial Society', *Proceedings of the American Philosophical Society*, 95.
1956. 'The Amazing Decline of Mortality in Underdeveloped Areas', *American Economic Review*, 46.

DAVIS, K., and BLAKE, J., 1956. 'Social Structure and Fertility: an Analytic Framework', *Economic Development and Cultural Change*, 4.

DEEVEY, E. S., 1960. 'The Human Population', *Scientific American*.

DUBLIN, L. I., LOTKA, A. J., and SPIEGELMAN, M., 1949. *Length of Life: A Study of the Life Table*. New York.

DURAND, J. D., 1958. 'World Population: Trends and Prospects', *Population and World Politics* by P. M. Hauser. Glencoe, Ill.

FABRICANT, S., 1958. *Basic Facts on Productivity Change*. National Bureau of Economic Research, Occasional Paper, 63. New York.

FAIRSERVIS, W. A., 1956. 'Excavations in the Quetta Valley, West Pakistan', *Anthropological Papers of the American Museum of Natural History*, 45, Part 2. New York.
1959. *The Origin of Oriental Civilization*. New York.

FEBVAY, M., and CROZE, M., 1954. 'Nouvelles données sur la mortalité infantile', *Population*, 9.

FORBES, R. J., 1958. *Man, the Maker*. London, New York.

FORD FOUNDATION, 1959. *India's Food Crisis*. Delhi.

FORDE, C. D., 1955. *Habitat, Economy and Society*. London.

FOURASTIÉ, J., 1949. *Le Grand Espoir du XX siècle*. Paris.

FRANKFORT, H., 1951. *The Birth of Civilization in the Near East*. London.

FROMM, E., 1956. *The Sane Society*. London.

GENICOT, L., 1953. 'Sur les témoignages d'accroissement de la population en Occident du XI au XIII siècle', *Cahiers d'histoire mondiale*, 1.

120

BIBLIOGRAPHY

GILBERT, M., *and associates*, 1958. *Comparative National Products and Price Levels*. Paris.

GILLE, B., 1954. 'Le Moulin à eau, une révolution technique mediévale', *Techniques et civilisations*, 3.

1956, 'Les Développements technologiques en Europe de 1100 à 1400', *Cahiers d'histoire mondiale*, 3.

GORDON CHILDE, V., 1955. *Man Makes Himself*. New York.

1958. *The Prehistory of European Society*. Harmondsworth.

GOSH, D., 1946. *Pressure of Population and Economic Efficiency in India*. Oxford.

HALL, A. R., 1954. *The Scientific Revolution*. London, New York.

HARE, R., 1954. *Pomp and Pestilence*. London.

HAUDRICOURT, A. G., 1936. 'De l'origine de l'attelage moderne', *Annales d'histoire économique et sociale*, 8.

HEICHELHEIM, F. M., 1956. 'Man's Role in Changing the Face of the Earth in Classical Antiquity', *Kyklos*, 9.

HELLEINER, K. F., 1957. 'The Vital Revolution Reconsidered', *Canadian Journal of Economics and Political Science*, 23.

HENRY, L., 1957. 'La Mortalité d'après les inscriptions funéraires', *Population*, 12.

1959, L'Âge du décès d'après les inscriptions funéraires', *Population*, 14.

HOWELLS, W., 1954. *Back of History*. New York.

1959. *Mankind in the Making*. New York.

HUXLEY, A., 1958. *Brave New World Revisited*. New York.

HUXLEY, J., 1957. *New Bottles for New Wine*. New York.

I.L.O., 1956. 'La Population active dans le monde : répartition par secteurs économiques', *Revue internationale du travail*, 73.

IVERSEN, J., 1941. 'Land Occupation in Denmark's Stone Age', *Danmarks Geologiske Undersogelse*, 66.

KANTNER, J. F., 1950. 'Recent Demographic trends in the U.S.S.R.', *Population Trends in Eastern Europe, the U.S.S.R. and Mainland China*. New York.

KENDRICK, J. W., 1956. *Productivity Trends: Capital and Labor*. National Bureau of Economic Research, Occasional Paper, 53. New York.

KENYON, K. M., 1957. Reply to Professor Braidwood, *Antiquity*, 31.

1959. 'Earliest Jericho', *Antiquity*, 33.

BIBLIOGRAPHY

KEYS, A., 1958. 'Minimum Subsistence', *The Population Ahead* (ed. R. G. Francis). Minneapolis.

KIRK, D., 1946. *Europe's Population in the Interwar Years*. League of Nations.

KROEBER, A. L., 1948. 'Summary and Interpretations' in 'A Reappraisal of Peruvian Archaeology' (ed. W. C. Bennett), *American Antiquity*, 13, 4, Part II.

KRZYWICKI, L., 1934. *Primitive Society and its Vital Statistics*. London.

KUCZYNSKI, R. R., 1934. 'Population', *Encyclopaedia of Social Sciences*.

KUZNETZ, S., 1946. *National Income, a Summary of Findings*, New York.

1952. 'Long Term Changes in the National Income of the United States of America since 1870', *Income and Wealth*, series 2. Cambridge.

1956. 'Quantitative Aspects of the Economic Growth of Nations', *Economic Development and Cultural Change*, 5.

1959. *Economic Growth*. Glencoe, Ill.

LE BARON BOWEN, R., 1960. 'Egypt's earliest sailing ships', *Antiquity*, 34.

LEFEBVRE DES NOÈTTES, R., 1931. *L'Attelage et le cheval de selle à travers les âges*. Paris.

LEIBENSTEIN, H., 1957. *Economic Backwardness and Economic Growth*. New York.

MACKENROTH, G., 1953. *Bevölkerungslehre*. Berlin.

MANGELSDORF, P. G., 1954. 'New Evidence on the Origin and Ancestry of Maize', *American Antiquity*, 19.

MASON, J. ALDEN, 1957. *The Ancient Civilizations of Peru*. Harmondsworth.

MATHER, K. M., 1944. *Enough and to Spare*. New York.

MINKES, A. L., 1955. 'Statistical Evidence and the Concept of Tertiary Industry', *Economic Development and Cultural Change*, 3.

MOLS, R., 1955. *Introduction à la démographie historique des villes d'Europe du XIV au XVIII siècle*. Louvain.

MORITZ, L. A., 1958. *Grain Mills and Flour in Classical Antiquity*. Oxford.

NEF, J. U., 1954. *La Naissance de la civilisation industrielle*. Paris.

NOUGIER, L. R., 1950. *Les Civilisations campigniennes en Europe Occidentale*. Le Mans.

BIBLIOGRAPHY

OAKLEY, K., 1955. 'Fire as Paleolithic Tool and Weapon', *Proceedings of the Prehistoric Society*, 21.
1956. 'The Earliest Fire Makers', *Antiquity*, 30.

O.N.U., 1956. 'Besoin du monde en énergie en 1975 et en l'an 2000', *Actes de la conférence internationale sur l'utilisation de l'énergie atomique à des fins pratiques*. Geneva.

ORTEGA Y GASSET, J., 1932. *The Revolt of the Masses*. New York.

OSTWALD, W., 1909. *Energetische Grundlagen der Kulturwissenschaft*. Leipzig.

PARETTI, V., and BLOCH, G., 1956. 'Industrial Production in Western Europe and the United States 1901 to 1955', *Banca Nazionale del Lavoro, Quarterly Review*, 39.

PEARL, R., 1925. *The Biology of Population Growth*. New York.

P.E.P. (ed.), 1956. *World Population and Resources*. London.

PIGGOTT, S., 1954. *The Neolithic Cultures of the British Isles*. Cambridge.

PING-TI HO, 1959. *Studies on the Population of China*. Cambridge, Mass.

PIRENNE, J., 1950. *Les Grands Courants de l'histoire universelle*. Paris.

PUTNAM, P. C., 1950. *The Future of Land Based on Nuclear Fuels*. Oak Ridge.
1953. *Energy in the Future*. New York.

PYKE, M., 1950. *Industrial Nutrition*. London.

RATZEL, F., 1891. *Anthropogeographie*. Stuttgart.

RUSSELL, J. C., 1958. 'Late Ancient and Medieval Population', *Transactions of the American Philosophical Society*, N.S., 48, III.

SAINT-EXUPÉRY, 1939. *Terre des hommes*. Paris.

SARKAN, N. K., 1957. *The Demography of Ceylon*. Ceylon.

SAUER, C. O., 1952. *Agricultural Origins and Dispersal*. New York.

SAUVY, A., 1958. *De Malthus à Mao Tse-Tung*. Paris.

SCHURR, S. H., and NETSCHERT, B. C., 1960. *Energy in the American Economy*, Baltimore.

SPENGLER, J. J., 1956. 'Basic data on economic development', *Population Theory and Policy* (ed. J. J. Spengler and O. D. Duncan). Glencoe, Ill.

STENDHAL, 1925. *Racine et Shakespeare*. Paris.

STOLNITZ, G. J., 1954-5. 'A Century of International Mortality Trends', *Population Studies*, 8.

BIBLIOGRAPHY

TA CHEN, 1946. *Population in Modern China*. Chicago.

TAEUBER, I. B., 1956. 'Population Growth in South East Asia', *Demographic Analysis* (ed. J. J. Spengler and O. D. Duncan). Glencoe, Ill.

TAYLOR, K. W., 1956. 'Some Aspects of Population History', *Demographic Analysis* (ed. J. J. Spengler and O. D. Duncan). Glencoe, Ill.

THIRRING, H., 1958. *Energy for Man*. Bloomington, Indiana.

TINBERGEN, J., 1942. 'Zur Theorie der langfristigen Wirtschaftsentwicklung', *Weltwirtschaftliche Archiv*, 55.

1956. *Economic Policy: Principles and Design*. Amsterdam.

TOYNBEE, A. J., 1960. 'Education: The Long View', *Saturday Review*.

U.N., 1953. *The Determinants and Consequences of Population Trends*. New York.

1958. *Recent Trends in Fertility in Industrialized Countries*. New York.

UNESCO, 1957. *World Illiteracy at Mid-century*. Paris.

U.S. BUREAU OF CENSUS, 1960. *Historical Statistics of the U.S.* Washington D.C.

USHER, A. P., 1959. *A History of Mechanical Inventions*. Boston, Mass.

VALLOIS, H. V., 1937. 'La Durée de la vie chez l'homme fossile', *Anthropologie*, 47.

VARAGNAC, A. (ed.), 1959. *L'Homme avant l'écriture*. Paris.

WEIDENREICH, F., 1949. 'The duration of life of fossil man in China and the pathological lesions found in his skeleton', *The Shorter Anthropological Papers of Franz Weidenreich*. New York.

WHITE, L. T., 1940. 'Technology and Invention in the Middle Ages', *Speculum*, 15.

WHITE, W. H., 1956. *The Organization Man*. New York.

WOLFE, A. B., 1933. 'The Fecundity and Fertility of Early Man', *Human Biology*.

WOOLLEY, C. L., 1929. *The Sumerians*. Oxford.

ZEUNER, F. E., 1956. 'The Radiocarbon Age of Jericho', *Antiquity*, 30.

1958. *Dating the Past*. London.

ZIMMERMANN, E. W., 1951. *World Resources and Industries*. New York.

Index

INDEX